DO-IT-YOURSELF

Home Networking

FOR

DUMMIES®

by Lawrence C. Miller

WILEY

Wiley Publishing, Inc.

Home Networking Do-It-Yourself For Dummies®

Published by
Wiley Publishing, Inc.
111 River Street
Hoboken, NJ 07030-5774
www.wiley.com

WILEY

About the Author

Lawrence Miller, CISSP, has worked in information security and technology management for 20 years. He is currently the Director of IT for a sports and event retail merchandising company and recently completed his MBA at Indiana University — Kelley School of Business. He has previously worked as the IT Operations Manager in a large U.S. law firm and as a consultant to various industries in the U.S. and Japan, and was a Chief Petty Officer in the U.S. Navy. Larry has written several other For Dummies books covering numerous topics, including information security and unified communications.

Dedication

To Michelle Louise Kirkiewicz — if beauty were only skin deep, you would be the most thick-skinned woman I had ever known. But true beauty is in the heart, and you are truly the most beautiful woman I have ever loved.

Author's Acknowledgments

Thank you to all the wonderful people at Wiley I have worked with on so many projects over the years. You all make writing so enjoyable and fulfilling: Amy, Blair, Carrie, Dan, . . . E, F, G, . . . Heidi, I, Jen, Katie, Laura, Mike, N, O, Paul, . . . Q, Rev, Susan, . . . T, U, V, . . . W, X, Y, and Zoe!

Publisher's Acknowledgments

We're proud of this book; please send us your comments at http://dummies.custhelp.com. For other comments, please contact our Customer Care Department within the U.S. at 877-762-2974, outside the U.S. at 317-572-3993, or fax 317-572-4002.

Some of the people who helped bring this book to market include the following:

Acquisitions and Editorial

Project Editor: Blair J. Pottenger

Acquisitions Editor: Amy Fandrei

Copy Editor: Heidi Unger

Technical Editor: Dan DiNicolo

Editorial Manager: Kevin Kirschner

Editorial Assistant: Amanda Graham

Sr. Editorial Assistant: Cherie Case

Cartoons: Rich Tennant (www.the5thwave.com)

Composition Services

Project Coordinator: Sheree Montgomery

Layout and Graphics: Claudia Bell, Joyce Haughey, Christin Swinford

Proofreader: Susan Hobbs

Indexer: WordCo Indexing Services

Publishing and Editorial for Technology Dummies

Richard Swadley, Vice President and Executive Group Publisher

Andy Cummings, Vice President and Publisher

Mary Bednarek, Executive Acquisitions Director

Mary C. Corder, Editorial Director

Publishing for Consumer Dummies

Diane Graves Steele, Vice President and Publisher

Composition Services

Debbie Stailey, Director of Composition Services

Table of Contents

Introduction

●●

Fifty years ago, most households had only one television and one telephone. As the price of these technological marvels dropped, families began purchasing additional televisions and telephones — and the home network was born!

Think about it: Your televisions are basically networked together on a cable network. Okay, not a perfect analogy — in the early days you had rabbit ears, which are more of a wireless network except it's not exactly a network. Your telephones are wired together in serial — multiple phones with one gateway (your telephone number).

In the not too distant past, the home computer sat on a desk in a study or family room and everyone went to the computer to use it. Today, computers have become the next technological commodity, and it is not uncommon to have multiple computers in a single household. And with wireless networks, the computer goes with you to wherever it's most convenient for you to use.

From being able to watch your favorite TV show or answer the telephone from any room in the house to doing work in a home office, networks are all about convenience.

This book helps you set up your home network — the computer kind, not the television or telephone type! I show you how to connect to the Internet, connect your computers and other devices, share files and music, secure your network, and much more!

About This Book

This book is designed to be a hands-on, practical guide to home networking. It's chock-ful of helpful screenshots and step-by-step instructions to guide you through basic and advanced home networking configuration tasks, and it provides just enough background information to help you understand what you're doing and why.

Each chapter is written as a stand-alone chapter, so feel free to skip over some chapters and go directly to the topics that most interest you. Don't worry; you won't get lost in some complex storyline, and you won't discover "whodunit" if you start at the end of the book and work your way back!

Foolish Assumptions

If you're reading this book, it's probably safe to assume you're interested in home networking and need some help getting started. Beyond that, I assume you have at least one computer running Microsoft Windows 7, an Internet service provider, and a can-do spirit to go along with your do-it-yourself character!

A basic working knowledge of computers and Windows operating systems (not necessarily Windows 7) is also helpful. If you need help with basic topics such as booting up your computer, connecting peripheral devices (including monitors, keyboards, and printers), and navigating around Windows (for example, you have no idea what the Control Panel or Windows Explorer is), I strongly recommend starting with a book such as Dan Gookin's *PCs For Dummies, Windows 7 Edition* or Andy Rathbone's *Windows 7 For Dummies* (both by Wiley) before attempting to set up your own home network.

Finally, the Time Needed at the beginning of each task throughout this book is an estimate. It assumes that you will read every screen and take the time to familiarize yourself with the various options available. Thus, if a task says it will take you 10 minutes to complete, it's possible that it may take you only two minutes — but these are estimates based on an average reader and an average computer user (that perhaps takes time to smell the roses!).

How This Book Is Organized

This book is comprised of the five parts described in the following paragraphs. Each chapter begins with some helpful background information about the topics that are discussed in the chapter. After the background information, I walk you through the various tasks step by step in an easy-to-follow, do-it-yourself format. I've also included helpful screenshots to guide you through the steps.

Part I: Doing Your Homework

You probably already have some idea of why you want a home network. In Chapter 1, I describe some of the many uses of a home network, possibly give you a few new ideas and different possibilities, and help you justify the expenditure, if necessary, to your Chief Financial Officer (spouse). Chapter 2 introduces you to some basic networking terms and concepts to help you talk the talk!

Part II: Installing Your Home Network

In Part II, I show you how to set up your home network, including how to install various networking equipment. Read Chapter 3 to learn about wired networks, or Chapter 4 to find out about wireless networks. Or read both chapters so you can build a hybrid network — but don't go bragging to your neighbors about how environmentally friendly your home network is; I'm talking about a wired and wireless combination network here!

Part III: Setting up Your Windows 7 Network

Next, it's time to set up all the bells and whistles! In Part III, I take you through various Windows 7 networking topics and show you how to set it all up. This includes setting up different user accounts (Chapter 5), creating a homegroup (Chapter 6), sharing network resources such as storage and printing (Chapter 7), connecting to the Internet (Chapter 8), connecting to your home network when you're away or to your office network from home — if that's allowed (Chapter 9) — and some fun stuff like networking your gaming system and home theater (Chapter 10).

Part IV: Keeping Your Network Safe and Healthy

In Part IV, I cover some very important topics that will help you keep your network running efficiently, protect your privacy, and keep your family safe. In Chapter 11, you learn about the Action Center, which you use to centrally manage your home network security. Next, in Chapter 12, I cover various Internet threats, how to recognize them, and how to protect your home network, and then I show you how to configure Windows Firewall and Windows Defender to protect your computers from Internet threats. In Chapter 13, I show you how to set up Windows Update to keep your computer current with the latest security patches and bug fixes. In Chapter 14, I cover backing up and restoring your important data — in case a hard drive ever crashes, a virus infects your PC, you accidentally delete a file, or worse. Finally, in Chapter 15, I cover some advanced security topics that you need to be aware of if you use your home network for a small business or home office.

Part V: The Part of Tens

Part IV includes some very short but helpful chapters that provide a handy reference in that familiar For Dummies format — the Part of Tens! I point you to ten handy resources that cover Windows 7 topics beyond home networking, in Chapter 16. In Chapter 17, I give you ten tips for addressing issues joining a homegroup, and in Chapter 18, I help you troubleshoot some common networking issues.

Icons Used In This Book

Throughout this book, I occasionally use icons to call attention to important information that is particularly worth noting. But don't bother trying to double-click any of them with your mouse! Here's what to look for and what to expect.

Thank you for reading; hope you enjoy the book — please take care of your writers. Seriously, this icon points out helpful suggestions and useful nuggets of information that may just save you some time and headaches.

This icon points out information or a concept that may well be worth committing to your nonvolatile memory, your gray matter, or your noggin — along with anniversaries, birthdays, and other important stuff!

"Danger, Will Robinson!" This icon points out potential pitfalls and easily confused or difficult-to-understand terms and concepts.

If you're an insufferable insomniac or vying to be the life of a World of Warcraft party, take note. This icon explains the jargon beneath the jargon and is the stuff legends — well, at least nerds — are made of.

Where to Go From Here

Well, if you had pointy ears instead of a pointy chin (like the Dummies Man logo), you might say, "Logic clearly dictates that you turn the page and start at the beginning." Instead, I suggest that the needs of *you* outweigh the needs of the *many,* and I've written this book to meet your needs. So turn the page and get started!

Part I
Doing Your Homework

The 5th Wave   By Rich Tennant

"Wait a minute...This is a movie, not a game?! I thought I was the one making Keanu Reeves jump kick in slow motion."

In this part . . .

Don't worry — it isn't a graded assignment! But you
do need to know why you're building a home network and understand some basics about networking
before you get started. So in this part, I help you explore
the possibilities for your home network, explain some networking terms and concepts, and describe some basic
networking equipment.

Chapter 1

Why Do You Need A Home Network?

Computer networks allow you to easily share resources with others. These resources may include Internet access, shared files and folders, printers, and much more. In this chapter, you explore the benefits of creating your own home network.

A Network by Any Other Name

A *network* is a group of computers that communicate with each other in order to share resources, such as Internet access, computing power, files and folders, printers, and even the computers themselves.

If you've worked on a corporate or office network, you may have heard the network referred to as the *LAN,* which is simply a *local area network.* Your home network can also be correctly described as a LAN. There is no hard and fast rule for how small or large a network must be in order to be considered a LAN. It may consist of as few as two computers or as many as several hundred computers.

Another acronym you may hear when referring to a network is *WAN*, or *wide area network*, which connects multiple networks together. For example, a corporation may connect several of its locations together on a private WAN. The biggest example of a WAN is the Internet, which connects networks as small as one computer to as large as thousands of computers together over the Internet.

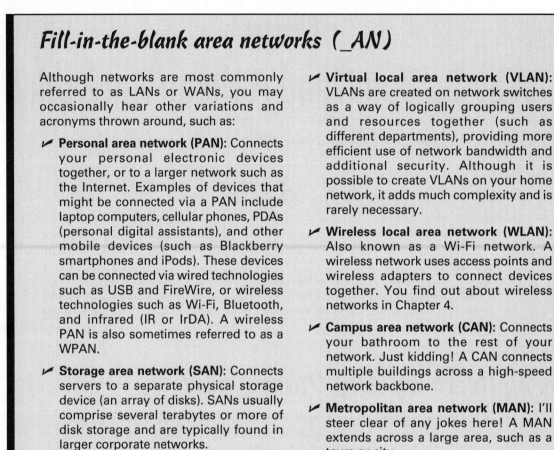

Fill-in-the-blank area networks (_AN)

Although networks are most commonly referred to as LANs or WANs, you may occasionally hear other variations and acronyms thrown around, such as:

- **Personal area network (PAN):** Connects your personal electronic devices together, or to a larger network such as the Internet. Examples of devices that might be connected via a PAN include laptop computers, cellular phones, PDAs (personal digital assistants), and other mobile devices (such as Blackberry smartphones and iPods). These devices can be connected via wired technologies such as USB and FireWire, or wireless technologies such as Wi-Fi, Bluetooth, and infrared (IR or IrDA). A wireless PAN is also sometimes referred to as a WPAN.

- **Storage area network (SAN):** Connects servers to a separate physical storage device (an array of disks). SANs usually comprise several terabytes or more of disk storage and are typically found in larger corporate networks.

- **Virtual local area network (VLAN):** VLANs are created on network switches as a way of logically grouping users and resources together (such as different departments), providing more efficient use of network bandwidth and additional security. Although it is possible to create VLANs on your home network, it adds much complexity and is rarely necessary.

- **Wireless local area network (WLAN):** Also known as a Wi-Fi network. A wireless network uses access points and wireless adapters to connect devices together. You find out about wireless networks in Chapter 4.

- **Campus area network (CAN):** Connects your bathroom to the rest of your network. Just kidding! A CAN connects multiple buildings across a high-speed network backbone.

- **Metropolitan area network (MAN):** I'll steer clear of any jokes here! A MAN extends across a large area, such as a town or city.

A Home Network for Everyone

Fifty years ago, most homes had only one television and one telephone at best. Just 20 years ago, most homes had only one computer, if any at all. Now, as computer prices have plummeted, homes commonly have a computer for practically every member of the family. The benefits of a home network include the following:

- **Sharing high-speed Internet:** In the not-too-distant past, sharing an Internet connection across multiple computers would have been laughable. Dialup modems, accompanied by their trademark symphony of screeches, beeps, and other harmonious sounds, are as aggravating as they are slow. With a top speed of about 56 Kbps over a traditional home telephone line, surfing the Internet is an exercise in patience. But as high-speed Internet with cable and DSL routers and modems has become more accessible (and affordable), sharing an Internet connection has become commonplace. (See Chapter 8 for more on connecting your home network to the Internet.)

✔ **Sharing files and printers:** Moving files over a home network is as easy as cutting and pasting, dragging and dropping, or pointing and clicking. A home network also makes it possible for you to share printers. No more tying up the "printer computer" to print a massive homework assignment or work project. (In Chapter 7, I tell you how to set up printer sharing.)

✔ **Playing games, videos, and more:** A home network allows multiplayer games, so you can enhance your game-playing experience well beyond Solitaire! You can also connect your digital video recorders (DVRs) and game consoles to your network to entertain the entire family (see Chapter 10).

A Home Network for One

A *network* is traditionally defined as two or more computers connected together. But even if you have only one computer, or you live alone, you may still find a home network beneficial. Wireless networks are ideal in both of these situations, particularly if you have a laptop computer. A wireless network with a laptop computer gives you the freedom to work from your desk, your bedroom, your kitchen, your backyard — just about anywhere in and around your home! And don't forget about the other wireless devices you may have, such as a game console and your mobile phone.

Building a SOHO: When Home and Office Become One

As home businesses and *telecommuting,* or working from home, have become more commonplace in today's business world, a small office or home office (SOHO) network is now a necessity for much of today's workforce. Much of the equipment for a SOHO network is the same as for a home network, but there are a few differences. For example, you may also need to connect a Voice-over-IP (VoIP) phone to your home network or set up a virtual private network (VPN), which I cover in Chapter 9. Depending on what type of work you're doing in your home office, you may also have regulatory compliance requirements (which I discuss in Chapter 15).

To Wire or Not To Wire

Your two choices for connecting computers in a network are wired and wireless. Wired networks are generally faster and more secure than wireless networks, but wireless networks provide mobility and convenience if you have laptop computers and mobile devices. If your home isn't prewired with Ethernet network cables (see Chapter 3), running network cables throughout your home can be a time-consuming chore and unsightly (imagine blue cables running along the walls and under rugs), unless you actually go through the trouble of running your cables behind walls and furniture.

Although a wired network generally provides faster network speeds than a wireless connection, that doesn't mean you'll get faster Internet speeds with a wired network. Wired networks typically operate at speeds of 100 or 1000 Mbps (megabits per second) and wireless networks operate in the 54 Mbps range. But a residential high-speed Internet connection typically provides only 5 Mbps of Internet bandwidth. So your bottleneck will almost always be your Internet connection, whether you have a wired or wireless network.

Of course, you don't have to be a purist when it comes to home networking. It's entirely possible to have a little bit of both, and this approach may be advantageous. For example, depending on the construction materials used in your home, you may find certain areas, such as your basement, difficult to cover with a wireless network. Running a network cable from your wireless router down to your basement, and connecting it to a hub or switch in the basement is one way to address spotty wireless coverage.

Both wired and wireless networks are fairly inexpensive to set up and require just a few basic pieces of networking equipment, which I explain in Chapters 3 (wired) and 4 (wireless).

Chapter 2

Understanding Networking Basics

Tasks Performed in This Chapter

▶ Getting familiar with basic Network properties

▶ Learning about IP addresses

▶ Addressing your network devices with DHCP

▶ Addressing your network devices manually

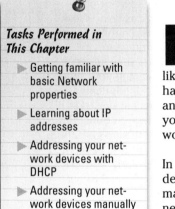

IP addresses, subnet masks, and default gateways form the logical building blocks of network devices. You have more than likely seen these settings on your computer before, but you may not have known what it all meant. More than likely, any time there was an issue with one of these settings, you got an error message telling you to contact your system administrator. Well, on your home network, that's you!

In this chapter, you learn enough about IP addresses, subnet masks, default gateways, and how to configure these network properties to make you dangerous — and get you up and running on your home network.

Understanding Basic Network Properties

To configure the various devices (such as computers, printers, routers, switches, and gaming consoles) on your home network, you need to know some basic information, including:

✔ IP address

✔ Subnet mask

✔ Default gateway address

✔ DNS server addresses

In the following sections, I explain what each of these network properties are, what they do, and how you obtain them. Then, I show you how to configure your network devices with all of these properties, both the hard way (manually) and the easy way (automatically)!

I'm not just showing you how to configure your network the hard way so that you can impress your geekiest friends! Unfortunately, not all network devices can be automatically configured, so you may need to know how to configure these properties manually.

IP addresses

Every device on a network must be uniquely identified with an *IP (Internet Protocol) address.* An IP address consists of four sets of numbers from 0 to 255, separated by a decimal, such as

```
192.168.1.200
```

Although the numbers in an IP address may appear random, there is a method to the madness. Each of the four numbers that comprise an IP address is known as an *octet* because it consists of 8 bits. With 8 bits, there are 256 possible combinations from 0 to 255.

IP addresses are assigned to *organizations* by the Internet Assigned Numbers Authority (IANA). That's right, organizations. So how do you, an *individual*, get your very own IP address? Your Internet service provider (ISP) can lease a permanent IP address to you, but that isn't really necessary, unless you're running your own Web or e-mail server on your home network. More often, your ISP dynamically assigns an IP address to you from a pool of addresses that IANA has assigned to your ISP. If your high-speed Internet connection is more or less always connected, you essentially get a permanent IP address anyway. Of course, there's no guarantee that you'll always get that same IP address (for example, if your router is reset or your ISP has a timeout set on your connection you may get a different IP address assigned), so if you're running your own Web or e-mail server, you'll need to get a permanent IP address from your ISP and manually configure it on your server. Otherwise, a dynamically assigned IP address is fine.

However, your ISP will give you only one IP address, and that one is assigned to your modem or router. You still need to assign a unique IP address to each of your network devices. Fortunately, IANA reserves three ranges of IP addresses for private use:

```
10.0.0.1 to 10.255.255.254
172.16.0.1 to 172.31.255.254
192.168.0.1 to 192.168.255.254
```

These IP addresses are never routed over the Internet, so you can use them on your home network as you see fit. But IP addressing can get very complicated very fast, so it's best to keep your IP numbering scheme as simple as possible. The easiest way to do this is to make the first three groups (or octets) of numbers in your IP address the same, and focus only on the last group. In the last group, start numbering the routers, computers, and other devices on your network from 1 to 254. For example, if you have the following devices on your network, you might assign them IP addresses as follows. (See Figure 2-1.)

Item	*IP Address*
Wireless router	192.168.1.1
Desktop PC (den)	192.168.1.2
Desktop PC (basement)	192.168.1.3
Laptop	192.168.1.4
Nintendo Wii	192.168.1.5

192.168.1.2

192.168.1.1

192.168.1.3

192.168.1.5

192.168.1.4

Figure 2-1: A simple IP addressing scheme.

Because private IP addresses cannot be routed over the Internet, your router or firewall must translate your private IP addresses to a public IP address (or IP addresses), which can be sent over the Internet. This is known as *Network Address Translation* (NAT) or *Port Address Translation* (PAT). NAT translates a private IP address (such as 192.168.1.2) to a public IP address (such as 71.156.85.214). PAT translates a range of private IP addresses (such as 192.168.1.2 to 192.168.1.254) to a single public IP address. Most home routers and firewalls sold today are preconfigured to perform NAT, or you can easily enable it, usually through a check box option or setup wizard depending on your router or firewall model.

Although NAT and PAT are distinctly different, the overall function (that is, translating IP addresses) is the same. Many router and firewall vendors do not distinguish between NAT and PAT in the user interface and simply refer to the address translation function as NAT.

Subnet masks

The second important piece of an IP address is the *subnet mask*. Similar to an IP address, the subnet mask consists of four numbers from 0 to 255 (but in the case of a subnet mask, only certain numbers within that range can be used), separated by decimal points. A subnet mask separates an IP address into two logical portions: a network portion and a host portion. The network portion identifies a unique network, and the host portion identifies an individual device on that network (such as a computer or printer). This is somewhat analogous to a 10-digit phone number, in which the first three digits represent the area code (or "network"), and the 7-digit phone number represents a unique phone line in that area (or "host"). But rather than limiting the Internet to 999 unique networks (a 3-digit area code only gives us 999 unique "areas"), a subnet mask allows you to have infinitely more unique networks by allowing the "area code" to be a variable number of digits within the IP address (for example, 3, 6, or 9, of the 12 total digits in an IP address). The subnet mask tells a computer or router how many of the digits in the IP address represent the network and how many of the digits represent unique devices (or "hosts") on the network.

A subnet mask can actually consist of far more combinations than just 3, 6, or 9 digits as described previously, but this oversimplification is sufficient for understanding the purpose of subnet masks.

Like IP addresses, subnet masks can get very complicated, very fast. The number 255 in a subnet mask essentially identifies the network portion of an IP address, while the number 0 essentially identifies the host portion of an IP address. For home networking purposes, it's usually sufficient to simply use a subnet mask of 255.255.255.0. Referring to the example in Figure 2-1, a subnet mask of 255.255.255.0 tells every device on your network that it belongs to the 192.168.1.0 network (the last 0 is just the default designation for a network; it is never actually assigned to a network device), and that the last number (1 through 5 in the previous example) is the unique host address.

This is a very simple description of IP addressing and subnet masks. Getting any fancier than this with your IP addressing scheme requires advanced networking knowledge and is rarely necessary on a home network.

Default gateway address

The default gateway, in most cases, is simply the IP address of your Internet router. Your router will typically have two IP addresses associated with it. One is the private IP address that you configure on your router (such as 192.168.1.1), and the other is the public IP address that your ISP assigns to your router — which can be a dynamic (temporary) or static (permanent) IP address. Although you can configure all of your network devices to use either the router's public or private IP address as the default gateway, it is usually best to use the private IP address (because the public IP address might change if it is not a permanently assigned static IP address from your ISP).

Continuing with the example in Figure 2-1, the *default gateway* address tells the various network devices how to get to an IP address that isn't on your local network. For example, if you're using your laptop and want to go to www.microsoft.com (IP address: 207.46.232.182), your laptop needs your router's help to get there. Rather than keeping track of every possible address on the Internet, your laptop simply hands the task to your router, whose job it is to find the best route to www.microsoft.com (among others). But how does your router know the IP address for www.microsoft.com (or any other Web site address for that matter)? That's the job of DNS, which I explain in the next section.

Domain Name System (DNS) server addresses

The Domain Name System (DNS) is the phonebook of the Internet. Although it's possible to surf the Internet without DNS by simply entering the IP address of the Web site you want to visit into your browser's address bar, it's not very practical. Just try memorizing the IP addresses of a few of your favorite Web sites, such as:

- ✔ www.facebook.com: (69.63.181.11)
- ✔ www.google.com: (74.125.229.51)
- ✔ www.microsoft.com: (207.46.232.182)
- ✔ www.wiley.com: (208.215.179.146)
- ✔ www.youtube.com: (74.125.227.39)

Or, save a few brain cells and let DNS keep track of it for you instead. A DNS server maps Web site names (such as www.microsoft.com) to IP addresses (such as 207.46.232.182) in a hierarchical format (analogous to a phonebook mapping names to phone numbers in an alphabetical format). Your ISP usually maintains its own DNS servers and provides several DNS server addresses to you as part of their service offering (just like your phone company provides you a phonebook). You normally configure a primary and secondary DNS server address on your network devices (just in case one of the DNS servers is busy or otherwise unavailable).

Manually Configuring Network Properties

Stuff You Need to Know

Toolbox:

- Computer running Windows 7
- IP address, subnet mask, default gateway address, and DNS server addresses
- Administrator account

Time Needed:
5 minutes

You can manually configure an IP address, subnet mask, and default gateway on all of the Windows 7 computers on your home network by following these steps:

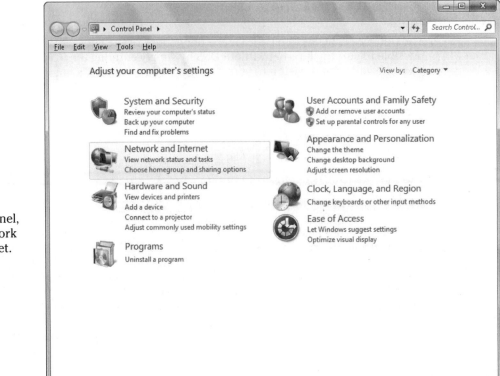

1. From the Control Panel, click Network and Internet.

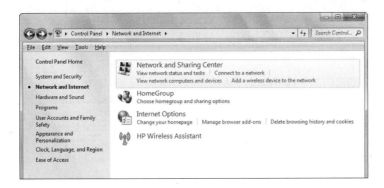

2. Click Network and Sharing Center.

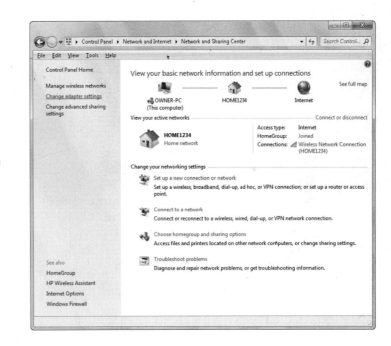

3. In the left pane, click Change Adapter Settings.

4. Double-click the network adapter you would like to configure (Wireless Network Connection in this example). The Wireless Network Connection Status dialog box appears.

Wireless Network Connection Status

General

Connection

IPv4 Connectivity: Internet
IPv6 Connectivity: No network access
Media State: Enabled
SSID: HOME1234
Duration: 02:09:10
Speed: 54.0 Mbps
Signal Quality:

Details...   Wireless Properties

Activity

Sent — Received

Bytes: 120,692   308,683

Properties   Disable   Diagnose

Close

5. Under Activity, click the Properties button.

Wireless Network Connection Properties

Networking

Connect using:

Intel(R) WiFi Link 1000 BGN

Configure...

This connection uses the following items:

☑ Client for Microsoft Networks
☑ Kaspersky Anti-Virus NDIS 6 Filter
☑ QoS Packet Scheduler
☑ File and Printer Sharing for Microsoft Networks
☑ Internet Protocol Version 6 (TCP/IPv6)
☑ Internet Protocol Version 4 (TCP/IPv4)
☑ Link-Layer Topology Discovery Mapper I/O Driver
☑ Link-Layer Topology Discovery Responder

Install...   Uninstall   Properties

Description

Transmission Control Protocol/Internet Protocol. The default wide area network protocol that provides communication across diverse interconnected networks.

OK   Cancel

6. In the next dialog box, select Internet Protocol Version 4 (TCP/IPv4) and click the Properties button.

7. In the Internet Protocol Version 4 (TCP/IPv4) Properties dialog box, select Use the Following IP Address and enter the IP address, subnet mask, and default gateway information for your network. I explain these values and how to obtain them earlier in this chapter.

```
┌─────────────────────────────────────────────────────────┐
│ Internet Protocol Version 4 (TCP/IPv4) Properties   [?][X]│
├─────────────────────────────────────────────────────────┤
│ ┌─ General ──────────────────────────────────────────┐  │
│                                                         │
│  You can get IP settings assigned automatically if your │
│  network supports this capability. Otherwise, you need  │
│  to ask your network administrator for the appropriate  │
│  IP settings.                                           │
│                                                         │
│  ○ Obtain an IP address automatically                   │
│  ◉ Use the following IP address:                        │
│     IP address:          192 . 168 . 0 . 2             │
│     Subnet mask:         255 . 255 . 255 . 0           │
│     Default gateway:     192 . 168 . 0 . 1             │
│                                                         │
│  ○ Obtain DNS server address automatically              │
│  ◉ Use the following DNS server addresses:              │
│     Preferred DNS server:    .   .                      │
│     Alternate DNS server:    .   .                      │
│                                                         │
│  ☐ Validate settings upon exit        [ Advanced... ]   │
│                                          [ OK ] [Cancel]│
└─────────────────────────────────────────────────────────┘
```

```
┌─────────────────────────────────────────────────────────┐
│ Internet Protocol Version 4 (TCP/IPv4) Properties   [?][X]│
├─────────────────────────────────────────────────────────┤
│ ┌─ General ──────────────────────────────────────────┐  │
│                                                         │
│  You can get IP settings assigned automatically if your │
│  network supports this capability. Otherwise, you need  │
│  to ask your network administrator for the appropriate  │
│  IP settings.                                           │
│                                                         │
│  ○ Obtain an IP address automatically                   │
│  ◉ Use the following IP address:                        │
│     IP address:          192 . 168 . 0 . 2             │
│     Subnet mask:         255 . 255 . 255 . 0           │
│     Default gateway:     192 . 168 . 0 . 1             │
│                                                         │
│  ○ Obtain DNS server address automatically              │
│  ◉ Use the following DNS server addresses:              │
│     Preferred DNS server:   192 . 168 . 0 . 1|         │
│     Alternate DNS server:    .   .                      │
│                                                         │
│  ☐ Validate settings upon exit        [ Advanced... ]   │
│                                          [ OK ] [Cancel]│
└─────────────────────────────────────────────────────────┘
```

8. Under Use the Following DNS Server Addresses, enter the IP addresses for your primary and secondary DNS servers. (Only a primary DNS server address is required. This may be the same address as your default gateway, or your ISP may provide you with this information.) Click OK and close the other network properties windows.

Automatically Configuring Network Properties

Stuff You Need to Know

Toolbox:
- ✔ Computer running Windows 7
- ✔ Administrator account

Time Needed:
5 minutes

The Dynamic Host Configuration Protocol (DHCP) allows you to automatically configure the network properties for most devices on your home network. Of course, you'll need to configure a DHCP server on your network (which I show you how to do in the next task). To configure your Windows 7 computer to use DHCP, follow these steps:

1. From the Control Panel, click Network and Internet.

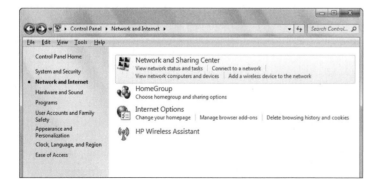

2. Click Network and Sharing Center.

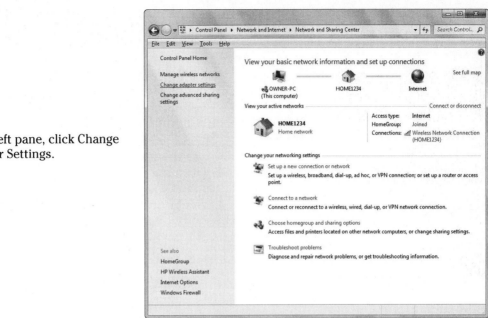

3. In the left pane, click Change Adapter Settings.

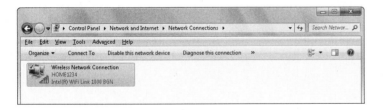

4. Double-click the network adapter you would like to configure (Wireless Network Connection in this example).

Wireless Network Connection Status

General

Connection

IPv4 Connectivity:	Internet
IPv6 Connectivity:	No network access
Media State:	Enabled
SSID:	HOME1234
Duration:	02:09:10
Speed:	54.0 Mbps
Signal Quality:	

Details...   Wireless Properties

Activity

	Sent — — Received
Bytes:	120,692 308,683

Properties   Disable   Diagnose

Close

5. Under Activity, click the Properties button.

Wireless Network Connection Properties

Networking

Connect using:

Intel(R) WiFi Link 1000 BGN

Configure...

This connection uses the following items:

- ☑ Client for Microsoft Networks
- ☑ Kaspersky Anti-Virus NDIS 6 Filter
- ☑ QoS Packet Scheduler
- ☑ File and Printer Sharing for Microsoft Networks
- ☑ Internet Protocol Version 6 (TCP/IPv6)
- ☑ Internet Protocol Version 4 (TCP/IPv4)
- ☑ Link-Layer Topology Discovery Mapper I/O Driver
- ☑ Link-Layer Topology Discovery Responder

Install...   Uninstall   Properties

Description

Transmission Control Protocol/Internet Protocol. The default wide area network protocol that provides communication across diverse interconnected networks.

OK   Cancel

6. In the next dialog box, select Internet Protocol Version 4 (TCP/IPv4) and click the Properties button.

7. In the Internet Protocol Version 4 (TCP/IPv4) Properties dialog box, select Obtain an IP Address Automatically and Obtain DNS Server Address Automatically. Click OK and close the other Network Properties windows.

8. Your computer is now configured to use DHCP and will be automatically (and seamlessly) configured with the correct IP address, subnet mask, default gateway, and DNS server addresses, each time you turn your computer on.

Internet Protocol Version 4 (TCP/IPv4) Properties

General | Alternate Configuration

You can get IP settings assigned automatically if your network supports this capability. Otherwise, you need to ask your network administrator for the appropriate IP settings.

◉ Obtain an IP address automatically
○ Use the following IP address:

IP address:
Subnet mask:
Default gateway:

◉ Obtain DNS server address automatically
○ Use the following DNS server addresses:

Preferred DNS server:
Alternate DNS server:

☐ Validate settings upon exit

Advanced...

OK | Cancel

Configuring Your DHCP Server

Stuff You Need to Know

Toolbox:

✔ Computer
✔ Router or Ethernet switch

Time Needed:
5 minutes

In order to configure your network devices using DHCP, you need to have a DHCP server on your network. You can run DHCP on practically any computer on your network, but because the DHCP server must be on for other devices on your network to get their IP address settings, it is often easiest to use the DHCP server that is built-in on most routers (either wired or wireless) and Ethernet switches because these devices are almost always left on. Although the steps for configuring the DHCP server will vary slightly depending on the hardware and software you are using, the following example, using a Netgear wireless router, gives you a good idea of what is required.

1. Access your router or switch using a browser window and log into the device (NETGEAR WGR614v7 wireless router in this example).

2. Under Advanced on the left side of the window, click LAN IP Setup.

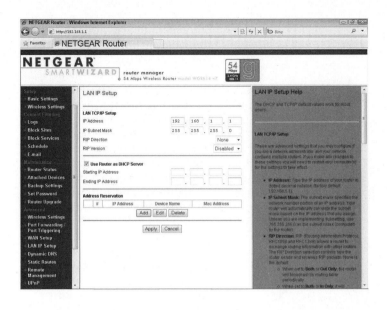

_3._ Select the check box next to Use Router as DHCP Server.

_4._ For the Starting IP Address, enter the first available host address in your IP address range. For example, if you manually configured your wireless access point with the IP address 192.168.1.1 (as in this example), the first available host address to be dynamically assigned would be 192.168.1.2. The host portion of the address is the number after the last decimal, so 2 would be the next available host address in this example. (The wireless access point in my example in this chapter has host address 1, represented as 192.168.1.1).

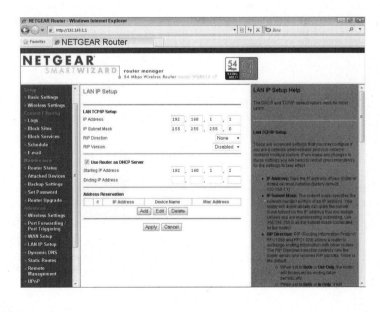

5. Enter an Ending IP Address within the same network range. You should allocate enough IP addresses to cover all the devices (for example, PCs and printers) on your network and a few extra for growth. For the most part, each device will require only one IP address. However, don't configure too many IP addresses. (The maximum is 254 in the example of a 192.168.1 network with host addresses from .1 to .254.) If you run out of IP addresses within your defined range, an IP address won't be available to assign to another device on your network, and it won't be able to connect to your network. Thus, IP address management is one additional method to limit access to your network, albeit not a very secure method. In this example, I've configured the Ending IP Address of 192.168.1.20 for a total of 20 host addresses (including the wireless access point).

6. Click Apply to save your settings.

DHCP is a first come, first serve protocol, so if your neighbor grabs the last available IP address on your network, you won't be able to connect to your own home network!

Part II
Installing Your Home Network

The 5th Wave   By Rich Tennant

"That's it! We're getting a wireless network for the house."

In this part . . .

Now it's time to roll up your sleeves and get your hands dirty — well, not that dirty! If you've already decided whether you want to build a wired or wireless network, you can skip directly to the appropriate chapter: Chapter 3 for wired, Chapter 4 for wireless. Otherwise, you can enjoy both chapters and then decide — or possibly do a little of both!

Part II
Installing Your Home Network

The 5th Wave   By Rich Tennant

"That's it! We're getting a wireless network for the house."

In this part . . .

Now it's time to roll up your sleeves and get your hands dirty — well, not that dirty! If you've already decided whether you want to build a wired or wireless network, you can skip directly to the appropriate chapter: Chapter 3 for wired, Chapter 4 for wireless. Otherwise, you can enjoy both chapters and then decide — or possibly do a little of both!

Chapter 3

Getting Wired

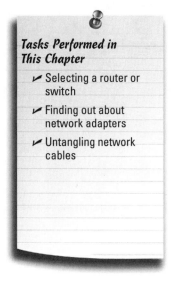

Tasks Performed in This Chapter

- ✔ Selecting a router or switch
- ✔ Finding out about network adapters
- ✔ Untangling network cables

Building a home network requires three basic pieces of hardware: a router, switch, network adapters, and network cables. If you've decided to build a wired home network, this chapter explains everything you need to know about the networking hardware you'll need.

Routers and Switches

The first important piece of networking hardware for your home network is a switch. A switch allows you to easily connect multiple computers and other network devices (such as printers) together (see Figure 3-1). You simply plug one end of an Ethernet cable into the network interface of your various devices and the other end into the switch.

A switch is a relatively simple piece of hardware. Home networking switches are commonly found in 4-port, 8-port, and 12-port configurations for generally less than $100. You will typically see a network switch identified as a 10/100 Ethernet or 10/100/1000 Gigabit Ethernet switch. This refers to the maximum network speed the switch will support *per connection*. Although you generally will want to connect your network devices at the highest possible speed, it is necessary to splurge on the fastest switch, particularly if cost is an issue. A 100-megabit Ethernet switch is more than enough for most home networking needs. NetGear, LinkSys (Cisco), and D-Link are three popular brands of home network switches. (See Figure 3-2.)

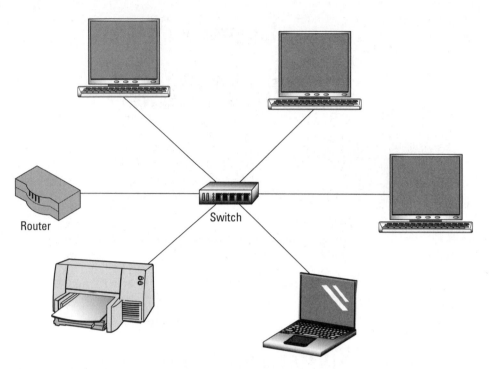

Figure 3-1: A switch connects multiple devices on a network.

Figure 3-2: A NetGear Ethernet switch.

There are a few variations of switches you should also be aware of when shopping for networking hardware. For example, a router with a built-in 4-port switch is one popular option. A router connects your home network to another network, such as the Internet. Having a built-in switch in your router saves you some hardware, space, and one extra electrical outlet! See Figure 3-3 for an example of a router with a 4-port switch.

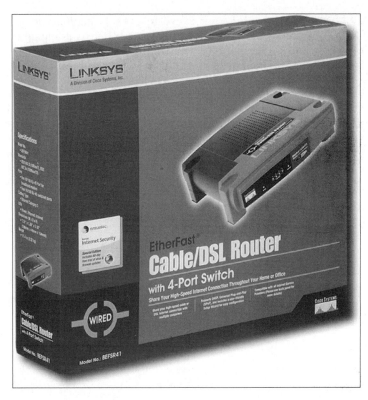

Figure 3-3: A LinkSys (Cisco) router with built-in 4-port switch.

A hub is another variation of a switch. Hubs and switches function in a similar manner, with one important difference:

- **Hub:** When a *hub* receives network traffic sent from one device to another, the hub broadcasts the traffic to all the devices on the network. The intended recipient processes the traffic, and all the other devices ignore the traffic. On small home networks, this difference is rarely a problem. However, broadcasting traffic through a hub can cause network congestion on busy networks, and because all devices connected to the hub see all of the traffic on the network, it is not particularly secure.

- **Switch:** A switch, on the other hand, is essentially an intelligent hub. A switch knows a little bit about the devices that are plugged into each of its ports and uses that information to send network traffic that it receives from one device, directly to the destination device. This causes less congestion on the network and is more secure than a hub.

Hubs used to be fairly common in small networks because they were relatively inexpensive. However, the price difference between hubs and switches has shrunk over the years to the point that there really is no reason to buy a hub today. A typical 4-port 10 Mbps hub costs about $30. By comparison, you can get a 4-port 10/100/1000 Mbps switch for about $50, and many wireless access points (see Chapter 4) and routers (discussed earlier, and in Chapter 8) have a built-in 4-port switch available for about $35 to $60.

It's also possible to forgo a switch altogether to create a (very) small home network. You can directly connect two computers to each other by plugging a crossover network cable into each computer's network adapter (known as a *computer-to-computer network*). You'll need an extra network adapter in at least one computer to link your home network to your Internet router (discussed in Chapter 8). This configuration allows you to connect two computers to the Internet with a shared network printer directly attached to one of the computers via a USB cable. To add more computers or (non-USB) devices, you'll need to add another network adapter to one of the computers. (See Figure 3-4.)

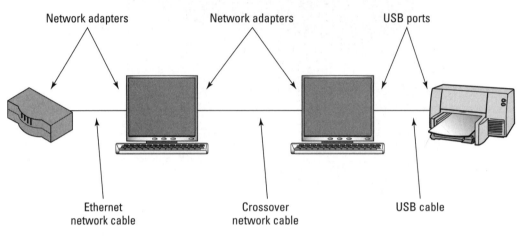

Figure 3-4: A computer-to-computer network.

 A crossover network cable crosses several transmit and receive wires in a cable so that two computers can be directly connected to each other. Newer network adapters can perform this "crossover" automatically, making crossover network cables less common today.

Identifying Network Adapters

Computers and other devices require a network adapter (or network interface card, NIC) to connect to and communicate on a network. The good news is that almost all desktop and laptop computers sold today have a built-in network adapter. Look for an input jack on the back of your desktop computer (or on the back or side of your laptop computer) that looks similar to a telephone input jack, but slightly wider.

 Many desktop and laptop computers also have a built-in modem. Don't confuse the modem jack with the network jack. The network jack is slightly wider than the modem jack and will usually have two small LED lights in the top corners of the jack. You should also see a small telephone symbol near the modem jack and a small network symbol (usually a horizontal line with several small squares, representing computers, along the line) near the network jack. See Figure 3-5.

Figure 3-5: A network jack (left) and modem jack (right) on the back of a laptop computer.

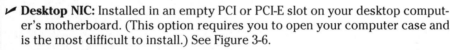

If your computer doesn't have a built-in network adapter or you need an additional one (if you're building a computer-to-computer network without a hub or switch, for example), you have several options. Network adapters are fairly inexpensive and are available in a variety of forms, such as:

✔ **Desktop NIC:** Installed in an empty PCI or PCI-E slot on your desktop computer's motherboard. (This option requires you to open your computer case and is the most difficult to install.) See Figure 3-6.

PCI (Peripheral Component Interconnect) and PCI-E (Peripheral Component Interconnect Express) are both computer expansion card standards. PCI-E is found on most newer computers.

Figure 3-6: A desktop NIC.

✔ **PC (or PCMCIA) Card:** A card (see Figure 3-7) about the same size as a credit card (but much thicker) that you insert into the PC (or PCMCIA) Card slot of your desktop or laptop computer.

PCMCIA Card was the original name for these types of cards. The abbreviation stands for Personal Computer Memory Card International Association. The name was later changed to PC Card, and they are now officially known as ExpressCards. Most people still refer to all of them as PCMCIA cards though.

Figure 3-7: A PC Card network adapter.

✔ **USB adapter:** A small device with a USB interface, typically the size of a thumb drive, that you plug into the USB port of any computer or network device with a USB port. See Figure 3-8.

Figure 3-8: A USB network adapter.

Ethernet standards

Ethernet is a networking standard that helps to ensure that all computer networking technologies from different vendors can work together on a network. The standard was developed in 1980 by the IEEE (Institute of Electrical and Electronics Engineers) and is officially known as the 802.3 standard. (You may recognize a pattern here — the 802.11 wireless standards, discussed in Chapter 4, are also defined by IEEE.)

Supported Ethernet standards are listed in the specifications and datasheets of various networking hardware and on the product packaging. Here's what to look for and what it all means:

✔ **10BASE-T:** Supports data rates up to 10 Mbps (megabits per second).

✔ **100BASE-TX:** Supports data rates up to 100 Mbps.

✔ **1000BASE-T:** Supports data rates up to 1000 Mbps (or 1 Gbps, gigabit per second).

If you think you've spotted a pattern here, you're absolutely correct! The first number (10, 100, or 1000 in these examples) denotes the speed in Mbps. *BASE* indicates that the cable uses *baseband signaling*, in which a single signal is transmitted over a wire, as opposed to *broadband signaling*, in which many signals across a wide range of frequencies are transmitted over a channel (or wire). Finally, *T* or *TX* indicates that it uses twisted-pair cables.

(continued)

(continued)

Warning: Do not confuse megabytes (MB) and megabits (Mb). Megabytes describe the amount of disk storage or memory. Megabits are used to describe the speed of a network connection (including your Internet connection). While mega- means the same thing in both terms — that is, 1000 — a byte is equivalent to 8 bits. So a megabyte is 8 times larger than a megabit.

Working with Network Cables

As you may have guessed, a key component in wired networks is — wires! More correctly, cables. The most common type of network cable in use today (and for the foreseeable future) is the twisted-pair Ethernet cable. Twisted-pair Ethernet cables are used to connect:

- ✔ DSL/cable routers or modems to computers
- ✔ DSL/cable routers or modems to wireless access points
- ✔ DSL/cable routers or modems to hubs or switches
- ✔ Computers to hubs or switches
- ✔ Computers to other computers
- ✔ Other devices (such as network printers) to computers, hubs, or switches

So what's the difference between a wire and a cable? A *wire* is a single conductor (typically copper) that may be solid or stranded. Two or more insulated wires grouped together in a sleeve or jacket (typically plastic) form a *cable*. (If each wire is not insulated, then it is technically still a wire.)

When purchasing network cables, you will most likely need Cat5e (or Cat6), UTP straight-through Ethernet cables with RJ-45 connectors in your preferred color and required length. I give you the details in the sections that follow.

Twisted pairs and RJ-45 connectors

Twisted-pair Ethernet cables consist of eight copper insulated wires in a plastic sleeve. Two wires are twisted together in a pair for a total of four pairs, and then the four pairs are twisted together to form the cable. The twists and pairs affect certain performance characteristics of the cable, such as *crosstalk*, *attenuation*, and *electromagnetic interference* (EMI).

Crosstalk occurs when an electrical signal transmitted over one wire negatively affects the electrical signal transmitted over another wire. *Attenuation* is the gradual loss of intensity of an electrical signal as it travels over the wire. *EMI* is noise (unwanted electrical signals) that is generated between the wires by the various electrical signals that are transmitted.

A clear plastic jack, known as an *RJ-45 connector,* is attached to both ends of the twisted-pair Ethernet cable. An RJ-45 connector looks very similar to a telephone jack (which, incidentally, is known as an *RJ-11 connector*). Figure 3-9 shows a twisted-pair Ethernet cable with RJ-45 connectors.

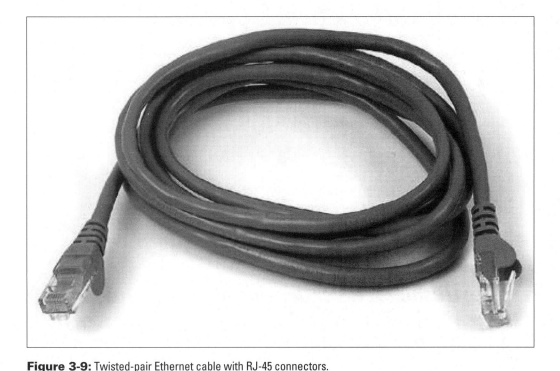

Figure 3-9: Twisted-pair Ethernet cable with RJ-45 connectors.

If you're wondering what RJ stands for, it's *registered jack.* And it's time to check your geek meter — it's pegged!

Twisted-pair Ethernet cabling is commonly referred to as simply Ethernet, Cat5, or UTP cable. Technically, *Ethernet* is a wiring and signaling standard that covers many types of cabling technologies; Cat5 is one category of several available categories (explained in the next section); and UTP is one of two possible types (explained in the upcoming "Unshielded versus shielded" section). However, these terms are commonly understood (albeit, incorrectly) to refer to twisted-pair Ethernet cabling.

Twisted pair categories

There are several categories of twisted-pair cabling, but only three that are commonly used for Ethernet networks: Category 5 (Cat5), Category 5e (Cat5e, or Cat5 Enhanced), and Category 6 (Cat6).

Cat1 (previously used in telephone, ISDN, and doorbell wiring), Cat2 (previously used on slower token ring networks), Cat4 (also previously used on token ring networks), and Cat5 (previously used on 100 Mbps Ethernet networks, and still commonly found) are no longer recognized as twisted-pair cabling standards. Cat3 is still considered a cabling standard for slower 10 Mbps Ethernet and telephone cabling. Cat6a, Cat7, and Cat7a are all newer standards for speeds up to 10 Gbps and are not used in home networks.

Although the *e* in Cat5e denotes *enhanced,* the *a* in Cat6a and Cat7a doesn't actually stand for anything — it just differentiates Cat6a and Cat7a from Cat6 and Cat7 cables.

The performance characteristics of Cat5, Cat5e, and Cat6 are as follows:

- ✔ **Cat5:** Supports speeds up to 100 Mbps at 100 MHz, with a maximum cable length of 328 feet (100 meters).

- ✔ **Cat 5e:** Supports speeds up to 1,000 Mbps (or 1 Gbps) at 100 MHz, with a maximum cable length of 328 feet (100 meters).

- ✔ **Cat6:** Supports speeds up to 1,000 Mbps (or 1 Gbps) at 250 MHz, with a maximum cable length of 295 feet (90 meters).

Unshielded versus shielded

Twisted-pair Ethernet cabling can also be *unshielded* (common) or *shielded* (not so common). *Unshielded twisted-pair* (UTP) cabling is used in both large enterprise networks and small home networks. It is relatively inexpensive and much more flexible than *shielded twisted-pair* (STP) cabling.

STP cabling is more expensive and less pliable than UTP cabling. It is used in industrial environments and other noisy environments (electrical noise; noisy kids or neighbors don't count) that are prone to high electromagnetic interference (EMI). The individual pairs of wires in STP cables are wrapped in foil or other metal shielding, and an outer metal shielding may also cover the entire group of twisted pairs (beneath the outer sleeve or jacket).

Straight-through versus crossover

In most cases, you will use straight-through twisted-pair Ethernet cables to connect the devices on your network. Crossover cables are sometimes required to directly connect two computers together (if one of them has a network adapter that is more than a few years old), to connect very cheap (or old) network switches that do not have an uplink port, or to connect some types of specialized network devices.

The difference between a straight-through and crossover cable is subtle but important. Two of the four pairs in a crossover cable are attached to the RJ-45 connector in a different order than in a straight-through cable, such that the transmitting and receiving wires are reversed. You can differentiate between a straight-through and crossover cable by looking at the wire pairs through the connector on either end of the cable (if you know the correct wiring order for straight-through and crossover cables). A crossover cable is sometimes labeled with an *X* on the cable near the connectors, and the cable sleeve is often red or yellow in color (although not always).

Do not assume that a red or yellow twisted-pair Ethernet cable is a crossover cable.

Length and color

The final two things you need to consider when choosing cables for your network are length and color.

Twisted-pair Ethernet cables come in a large selection of standard lengths, such as 3, 5, 7, and 10 feet. Longer lengths are available, and you can also have custom cable lengths made, up to the maximum length specified for the category of cabling you are using (for example, 328 feet). The distance between your various network devices and your network switch or router will determine the length you need. Don't forget to include enough length to run cables along walls, under rugs, and around corners as necessary.

Twisted-pair Ethernet cables come in all sorts of colors. This decision can be based purely on your individual tastes and preference. Blue is perhaps the most common, but you might also consider white, gray, or some other color that doesn't clash with your walls and carpet. Finally, you may want to stick with a single color for all the cables on your network.

Putting It All Together

Stuff You Need to Know

Toolbox:

- ✔ Router with built-in switch
- ✔ At least two network devices (for example, a computer and a printer) with network adapters
- ✔ At least two Ethernet network cables

Time Needed:

15 minutes

Now that you've got the router/switch, network adapters, and cables for all of your computers, printers, gadgets, and assorted doohickeys sorted out, it's time to connect it all together!

1. First, install your network switch or router. Connect the power adapter to the back of the switch or router, then plug the power cord into an electrical outlet or (preferably) a surge protector. If you have a router, see Chapter 8 for further configuration instructions.

2. Run your network cables along the walls, behind the furniture, and under the carpet as necessary from your network switch to your various computers and printers. ***Do not connect*** the cables to your network equipment yet — you don't want to accidentally jerk your network switch across the living room!

3. Once you have your network cables in place, connect one end of each network cable to a port on your network switch. You should hear a click when the network jack is properly inserted in the switch port. Connect the other end of the network cable to the network adapter ports of your computers and printers.

4. Turn your computers and printers on. Your network is now wired! Refer to Figure 3-1 for an example of your wired network.

Chapter 4

Going Wireless

Tasks Performed in This Chapter

- ✓ Defining your home networking needs
- ✓ Selecting the right wireless access point
- ✓ Configuring your wireless network
- ✓ Locking down your wireless network
- ✓ Connecting to your wireless network

Wireless (or Wi-Fi) home networks have become ubiquitous thanks to their ease of setup, convenience, and low cost. Virtually every laptop or netbook available today has a built-in Wi-Fi adapter. Multifunction printers, mobile devices, gaming systems, home theaters, and numerous other electronic accessories are increasingly sold Wi-Fi ready!

In fact, desktop PCs are pretty much the last bastion of wired holdouts, but that's not a problem either — most wireless access points and wireless routers (which I tell you about in this chapter) have several built-in ports for wired connections, or you can purchase a wireless adapter for your desktop PC for less than $100.

In this chapter, I show you how to design a wireless home network that fits your particular needs, set up your Internet connection, configure your wireless equipment, and keep the bad guys off your Wi-Fi network!

Planning Your Wireless Home Network

Building a wireless home network can be as simple as buying a wireless access point (WAP) — also known as an access point (AP), wireless router, or base station — and connecting it to your Internet router or modem. But, of course, it's rarely that simple. You should begin by asking yourself, "Self, what exactly do I want to do on my wireless network?" Some possible answers might be

- ✓ Surf the Internet, send and receive e-mails, blog, and chat online.
- ✓ Connect securely to a remote office network via a virtual private network (VPN). (See Chapter 9 to find out more.)
- ✓ Connect multiple PCs and other wireless devices (such as printers, home security systems, home theaters, and gaming systems).
- ✓ Conduct live meetings or webinars.
- ✓ Play network games with others online.
- ✓ Stream live music or video (including radio stations, TV, and movies).

✔ Make Internet phone calls (using Voice over IP, or VoIP).

✔ Send live video over the Internet. (Participate in video calls and videoconferences.)

✔ Share documents, music, photos, and videos with others over your network and the Internet.

✔ All of the above!

After you have an idea of some of the things you might want to do on your wireless network, you can determine how much speed you'll need, and I help you do that here. I also help you make sure you get the coverage you need and tell you what features might be available to you when you buy a wireless access point.

A wireless access point is typically used to connect your wireless devices (such as laptop PCs and gaming consoles) to wired devices (such as a server or Internet router) using an Ethernet switch (see Chapter 3). A wireless router is a wireless access point, that has a built-in router (to provide access to other networks, such as the Internet) and usually a 4-port Ethernet switch as well.

Speed

The more things you plan to do from the preceding list, the more speed you'll need. Not so incidentally, as you work your way down the list, your speed requirements generally tend to increase. For example, making a voice or video phone call over the Internet requires significantly more speed (and bandwidth) than connecting multiple PCs or sending a few e-mails.

The speed of your wireless network is important, but the speed of your Internet connection is usually more of a limiting factor when doing things on the Internet. Typical speeds for residential Internet access range from 768 kilobits per second (Kbps) to 1.5 megabits per second (Mbps) for DSL, and 4 to 6 Mbps for cable. High-end connections of up to 7 Mbps (DSL) and 20 Mbps (cable) are also available. By comparison, the most popular standard for wireless access points (802.11g) today provides speeds of up to 54 Mbps for connected devices.

The different types of wireless access points are generally classified according to a defined standard. The Institute of Electrical and Electronics Engineers (IEEE) defines the standard, known as 802.11. See Table 4-1 for a summary of the most common 802.11 wireless standards.

Table 4-1	Common 802.11 Wireless Standards		
Standard	*Frequency*	*Speed*	*Approx. Indoor Range*
802.11a	5 GHz	Up to 54 Mbps	50 feet
802.11b	2.4 GHz	Up to 11 Mbps	150 feet
802.11g	2.4 GHz	Up to 54 Mbps	150 feet
802.11n	2.4 or 5 GHz	Up to 300 Mbps	300 feet

802.11g is the most common standard in use today, and most built-in wireless adapters are 802.11g compatible. The maximum total speed possible on an 802.11g wireless network is 54 Mbps. This standard is also backward compatible with the 802.11b standard, which was previously the most common standard in the home wireless networking market.

As you connect more devices to your wireless network, less speed is available to each device, and network performance decreases overall. So while 54 Mbps may be all you need for one or two computers connected to your network, it's very easy to see how a network with three or four computers, a wireless printer, and a Nintendo Wii or Microsoft Xbox 360 (or both), can quickly outgrow an 802.11g wireless network.

It's also important to remember that while your Internet connection may be significantly slower than your wireless network, not all of your network traffic is Internet-based. For example, you might stream audio from the Internet to a single device on your network, and then multicast it to your home theater system in multiple rooms throughout your house. In this case, your wireless access point can easily become your network bottleneck.

802.11n is the newest wireless standard and is quickly becoming popular, with speeds of up to 300 Mbps (although up to 600 Mbps is the official standard). In addition to higher speeds, 802.11n can cover greater distances than the other 802.11 standards, it's backward compatible with 802.11b and 802.11g equipment, and it can operate at the 2.4 or 5 GHz frequency range.

Why does the frequency matter? Many cordless telephones and home appliances (such as microwave ovens) operate at the 2.4 GHz frequency range and can therefore interfere with wireless networks operating at 2.4 GHz. This interference can decrease the overall quality and performance of your wireless network.

Coverage

Another important planning consideration for your wireless network is coverage. Proper placement of your access point is crucial to maximizing the area your wireless network will cover. Oftentimes, it's just a matter of plugging in a single access point wherever it's convenient, but there are exceptions.

For example, if you have a very large home, you may not be able to cover your entire house with a single access point. You may decide you don't necessarily need coverage throughout your house, in which case you just need to find the best location for your access point to provide coverage in the rooms you need. Otherwise, you'll need to install more than one access point — which requires some additional configuration, such as assigning a different IP addresses to the wireless devices that connect to each access point to ensure two devices don't get the same IP address (I explain exactly what you need to do in the "Configuring Your Wireless Network" section later in this chapter).

Also, certain construction materials may interfere with your wireless signal, decreasing the signal strength and overall coverage. For example, thick concrete walls in your basement or apartment building may reduce coverage.

Although you can use a professional utility to help you determine the optimum placement for your access point and map your network coverage, generally it's easiest (and cheapest) to just experiment with a few different locations throughout your home. Plug your access point into an outlet in a few different rooms or closets (you don't even need to connect it to the Internet), and walk around your home with your laptop. Ensure your laptop can connect to your wireless network throughout your home (or the rooms you want covered) and that the signal is sufficiently strong (at least three "bars" on your wireless indicator, which is located in the system tray next to your clock in the lower right corner of your screen). Weaker signals degrade speed and performance. Although most wireless antennas are omnidirectional, you should experiment with your access point at different heights that are close to the approximate height you plan to place it. Inevitably, some characteristic of a wall or closet will cause your wireless signal to be different at 3 feet from the floor than it is at 3 feet from the ceiling.

Some general guidelines for placing your wireless access point in the optimum location include placing it

- Near the center of the area where you will be operating the majority of your wireless network PCs and equipment
- In an elevated location, for example on a high shelf
- Away from large metal or heavy concrete surfaces
- Away from potential sources of interference such as kitchen appliances and cordless phones

Finally, it's important to remember that maximum coverage is not always desirable. At greater distances from the access point, wireless signals are generally weaker and network speed decreases.

Also, your wireless signal will likely extend beyond the walls of your home. If your network is not properly secured, others will potentially be able to access private data on your home network and use your Internet connection. Even if you live on a farm and your nearest neighbor is miles away, you should secure your wireless network. You may recall the cautionary tale of Zuckerman's famous pig, Wilbur, who found an open access point and used it to send spam over Charlotte's World Wide Web. I explain how to secure your wireless network later in this chapter in the "Securing Your Wireless Access Point" section.

Less ominously, if your neighbors have wireless networks of their own — and they're installed with the default channel settings (which they most likely are, unless you recommend this book to all of your neighbors!) — it's possible that your wireless signals will interfere with each other's wireless networks and decrease the overall performance of all of your networks. I tell you about changing the channel later in the "Securing Your Wireless Access Point" task.

Buying a wireless access point

Now that you know what you want to do with your wireless home network and understand some of the fundamental differences between wireless standards, it's time to buy a wireless access point. Some popular brands include NETGEAR and Linksys. (See the examples in Figures 4-1 and 4-2, respectively.)

Figure 4-1: NETGEAR wireless access point.

Figure 4-2: Linksys wireless access point.

You can purchase a basic 802.11g wireless access point for as little as $35. An 802.11n access point goes for as little as $50. Various features and options available in different wireless access points may include

- ✔ **Built-in 10/100 switch:** Typically 4-port, to connect wired network equipment.

- ✔ **Dynamic Host Configuration Protocol (DHCP):** Automatically configures private Internet addresses for networked devices. I tell you more about DHCP in Chapter 2.

- ✔ **MAC address filtering:** Allows only specific devices to connect to your home network, based on the device's unique physical address, which is "burned in" to its wireless network adapter. I tell you more about MAC addresses in the "Connecting Your Wireless Access Point to the Internet" task later in this chapter.

- ✔ **Integrated DSL modem:** Connects directly to a DSL phone line for Internet access.

- ✔ **Integrated firewall:** Prevents unauthorized access from the Internet to your home network.

- ✔ **Content filtering or parental controls:** Blocks certain Web sites and restricts hours of access.

- ✔ **Built-in USB ports:** To quickly connect a USB device such as an external hard drive for shared storage.

- ✔ **Guest access:** Allows temporary, restricted access for visitors.

- ✔ **Quality of Service:** QoS, which prioritizes certain traffic, such as Voice over IP or streaming video.

Installing Your Wireless Access Point

Stuff You Need to Know

Toolbox:
- ✔ Computer
- ✔ Wireless access point
- ✔ DSL or cable modem
- ✔ Two Ethernet network cables
- ✔ Power adapter
- ✔ Internet connection

Time Needed:
10 minutes

After you've purchased your wireless access point, it's time to set it up! Begin by unpacking your wireless access point. In the box, you should find the wireless access point, a power adapter, and an Ethernet network cable.

An Ethernet network cable is simply a short cable (often about 3 feet in length) with a small connector that looks similar to, but slightly larger than, the connector you use to plug your phone into a wall jack.

To install a wireless access point, follow these steps:

1. Turn off your computer and modem.

2. If your modem is already connected to your computer with an Ethernet cable (often yellow in color), disconnect the cable end that is plugged into your computer and plug it into the Internet (or WAN) port of your wireless access point. Otherwise, connect the Ethernet port of your cable modem or router to your wireless access point's Internet (or WAN) port using an Ethernet network cable.

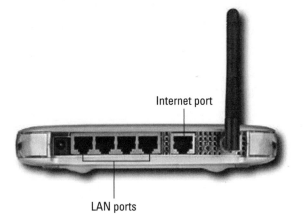

Internet port

LAN ports

TIP

The Internet (or WAN) port on a wireless access point is usually labeled or physically set slightly apart from the LAN ports.

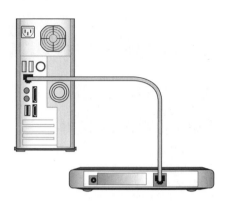

3. Connect your wireless access point to your computer using an Ethernet network cable. Plug one end of the cable into one of the LAN ports of your wireless access point and the other end to the Ethernet port on your computer.

4. Turn on your DSL or cable modem and wait about two minutes. This gives your modem enough time to boot up and establish a connection to the Internet. If you haven't connected your DSL or cable modem to the Internet, see Chapter 8.

5. Next, connect the power adapter to your wireless access point, plug it into an electrical outlet, and wait about one minute. This gives your wireless access point enough time to boot up, establish a connection to your modem, and begin broadcasting a wireless signal.

6. Finally, turn on your computer.

Your computer may have a built-in dialup modem with a phone port. Do not confuse the phone port with your Ethernet port. If your Ethernet cable doesn't fit the port, you've got the wrong port. Keep looking!

Configuring Your Wireless Access Point

After installing your wireless access point, you can configure it. To quickly configure your wireless access point with basic settings, you can use the CD that was included with your wireless access point. Insert the CD, and follow the instructions when it starts. If the CD doesn't start automatically, you can browse the CD contents in Windows Explorer and double-click Autorun or Setup.

Alternatively, you can open an Internet Explorer browser window. Many wireless access points in their factory default settings will automatically launch a setup wizard when you launch a Web browser. If not, you will need to enter the default address, which you can find in the instructions.

For this wireless router, the default login ID is *admin* and the default password is *password*. Your device's login credentials might be different, so be sure to read the setup instructions that are included with your wireless router. Once logged in, you can launch the Setup Wizard or, to manually configure your wireless access point, see the steps that follow. These are the steps to configure a NETGEAR WGR614v7 wireless router, but your steps may be a little different depending on the wireless device you're using.

Warning: Change the default password on your wireless access point as soon as possible; otherwise, a not-so-neighborly neighbor could log into your wireless access point and change your settings — thereby locking you out of your own network! If you are not automatically prompted to change it the first time you log in, look for a menu option to Set Password, Change Password, or Manage Accounts.

1. Under Setup on the left side of the window, click Basic Settings.

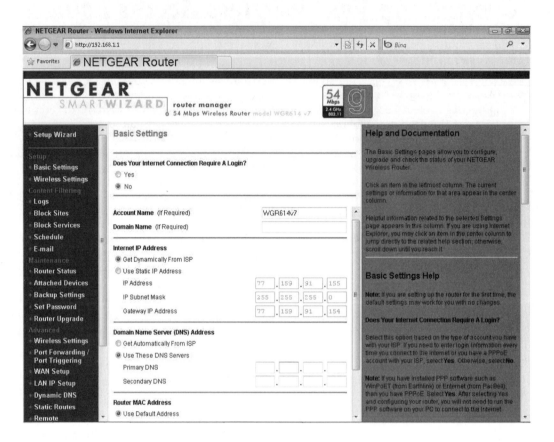

2. Refer to the Internet connection instructions provided by your Internet Service Provider (ISP). If your ISP does not require you to log in every time you connect to the Internet, select No under Does Your Internet Connection Require A Login and continue to Step 3. Otherwise, select Yes, choose your ISP from the drop-down menu (Other is the most common, in this example), enter the login and password information provided by your ISP (your login is most likely your e-mail address), and the service name (if required). If a service name is not required, simply leave it blank. Finally, you can enter an idle timeout (the period of inactivity, in minutes, after which your ISP automatically logs you off the Internet). Continue to Steps 3, 4, and 5 to configure your Internet IP address and domain name server (DNS) address before clicking the Apply and Test buttons on this screen.

Basic Settings

Does Your Internet Connection Require A Login?
- ⦿ Yes
- ◯ No

Internet Service Provider	Other ▾
Login	lmiller@myisp.net
Password	••••••••••••
Service Name (If Required)	
Idle Timeout (In Minutes)	5

Internet IP Address
- ⦿ Get Dynamically From ISP
- ◯ Use Static IP Address   0 . 0 . 0 . 0

Domain Name Server (DNS) Address
- ⦿ Get Automatically From ISP
- ◯ Use These DNS Servers
  - Primary DNS   ☐.☐.☐.☐
  - Secondary DNS ☐.☐.☐.☐

[Apply] [Cancel] [Test]

If you enter an Idle Timeout period of 0, your Internet connection will automatically reconnect every time your connection is lost.

If you have not previously set up your Internet connection, you should first attempt to connect with the default settings on your wireless access point (no login required for your Internet connection).

Basic Settings

Does Your Internet Connection Require A Login?

○ Yes

◉ No

Account Name (If Required) `WGR614v7`

Domain Name (If Required)

Internet IP Address

◉ Get Dynamically From ISP

○ Use Static IP Address

IP Address

IP Subnet Mask

Gateway IP Address

Domain Name Server (DNS) Address

○ Get Automatically From ISP

◉ Use These DNS Servers

Primary DNS

Secondary DNS

Router MAC Address

◉ Use Default Address

3. Under Account Name and Domain Name, enter your host or system name — and a domain name, if required (not common). Some ISPs require you to enter an account name, which may be the same as your Internet connection login ID (if login is required), or may be some other specific name assigned by your ISP, such as *home* or *ELA8435-B*. Likewise, your ISP may assign you a specific domain name, such as a workgroup name or the provider's domain name (for example, *earthlink.net*). Otherwise, you can leave this information blank.

4. Under Internet IP Address, select Get Dynamically from ISP. This is the most common configuration (and the easiest to set up). Every time you connect to the Internet, your ISP will automatically assign you an IP address and push the required connection information to your wireless router. Alternatively, if your ISP has assigned you a permanent static IP address (you have to pay your ISP more for this option), select Use Static IP Address and enter the IP address, IP subnet mask, and gateway IP address provided by your ISP.

Static IP addresses used to be more popular, particularly among people who wanted a permanent address they could use to connect back to their home network from anywhere. However, many applications (for example, GoToMyPC) now have the ability to find a computer, even if it uses a dynamic IP address.

An *IP address* uniquely identifies your computer on the Internet. The *IP subnet mask* divides the IP address into a network portion and a host portion. Subnet masking is a fairly complex topic. For home networking purposes, it is sufficient for you to understand that the value 255 refers to the network portion of your IP address, and the value 0 refers to the host portion. Finally, your *gateway IP address* is the address of the next hop on your network that gets you to the Internet. (Typically, the next hop is a router.)

Basic Settings

Does Your Internet Connection Require A Login?

- ○ Yes
- ◉ No

- ○ Use Static IP Address

IP Address	77	159	91	155
IP Subnet Mask	255	255	255	0
Gateway IP Address	77	159	91	154

Domain Name Server (DNS) Address

- ○ Get Automatically From ISP
- ◉ Use These DNS Servers

Primary DNS		.	. .
Secondary DNS		.	. .

Router MAC Address

- ◉ Use Default Address
- ○ Use Computer MAC Address
- ○ Use This MAC Address   `00:22:3F:3A:1A:F7`

[Apply] [Cancel] [Test]

5. Under Domain Name Server (DNS) Address, select Get Automatically from ISP. This is the most common configuration (and the easiest to set up). Otherwise, select Use These DNS Servers and enter the primary DNS and secondary DNS information provided by your ISP.

If you use a static IP address (see Step 4), you will most likely need to manually enter your DNS information by selecting Use These DNS Servers.

DNS is the phone directory, so to speak, of the Internet. Rather than memorizing the phone number of every person you know, you typically store their names and phone numbers on your phone (or for the truly nostalgic, you might look it up in a phone book). Similarly, rather than memorizing an address such as 207.46.197.32 and typing it into a Web browser every time you want to visit the Microsoft Web site, you simply need to type in www.microsoft.com, and DNS converts it to an IP address.

6. Under Router MAC Address, select Use Default Address. This is the most common configuration. If your ISP requires MAC authentication (extremely rare), select either Use Computer MAC Address or Use This MAC Address and enter the physical address of your PC's wireless LAN adapter.

   If you need to determine the physical address of your PC's wireless LAN adapter, right-click the Computer icon on your Windows 7 desktop and select Open Command Prompt Here. In the command prompt window that appears, type **ipconfig /all** and press Enter. The physical address is indicated on the third line below Wireless LAN Adapter Wireless Network Connection (00-26-C7-04-70-C4, in this example). Enter the physical address in the field next to Use This MAC Address, replacing hyphens (-) with colons (:).

```
C:\Windows\system32\cmd.exe

C:\>ipconfig /all

Windows IP Configuration

        Host Name . . . . . . . . . . . . : Owner-PC
        Primary Dns Suffix  . . . . . . . :
        Node Type . . . . . . . . . . . . : Hybrid
        IP Routing Enabled. . . . . . . . : No
        WINS Proxy Enabled. . . . . . . . : No

Wireless LAN adapter Wireless Network Connection:

        Connection-specific DNS Suffix  . :
        Description . . . . . . . . . . . : Intel(R) WiFi Link 1000 BGN
        Physical Address. . . . . . . . . : 00-26-C7-04-70-C4
        DHCP Enabled. . . . . . . . . . . : Yes
        Autoconfiguration Enabled . . . . : Yes
        Link-local IPv6 Address . . . . . : fe80::6ca3:b79a:4be4:48fc%13(Preferred)
        IPv4 Address. . . . . . . . . . . : 10.0.0.2(Preferred)
        Subnet Mask . . . . . . . . . . . : 255.255.255.0
        Lease Obtained. . . . . . . . . . : Monday, June 28, 2010 10:16:43 AM
        Lease Expires . . . . . . . . . . : Tuesday, June 29, 2010 8:01:19 AM
        Default Gateway . . . . . . . . . : 10.0.0.1
        DHCP Server . . . . . . . . . . . : 10.0.0.1
        DHCPv6 IAID . . . . . . . . . . . : 318777031
        DHCPv6 Client DUID. . . . . . . . : 00-01-00-01-13-04-31-87-C8-0A-A9-0D-FB-FB

        DNS Servers . . . . . . . . . . . : 10.0.0.1
        NetBIOS over Tcpip. . . . . . . . : Enabled
```

7. Click Apply, and then Test, to save and verify your settings.

The MAC (or physical address) of a device is sometimes referred to as the *burnt-in address* (BIA) because it is permanently burnt into the hardware (for example, a network adapter card). Like the IP address, the MAC address uniquely identifies a device, but it routes information across local area networks (LANs) using switches, rather than across wide area networks (WANs) using routers. MAC addresses use the hexadecimal numbering system (which is why it's so confusing just to look at it!).

Securing Your Wireless Access Point

Stuff You Need to Know

Toolbox:
- Computer
- Wireless access point (NETGEAR WGR614v7 in this example)

Time Needed:
10 minutes

After connecting your wireless access point to the Internet, it's time to configure the wireless settings so your wireless network devices (such as your computer and printer) can connect to your wireless network. To do so, follow these steps:

1. Under Setup on the left side of the window, click Wireless Settings.

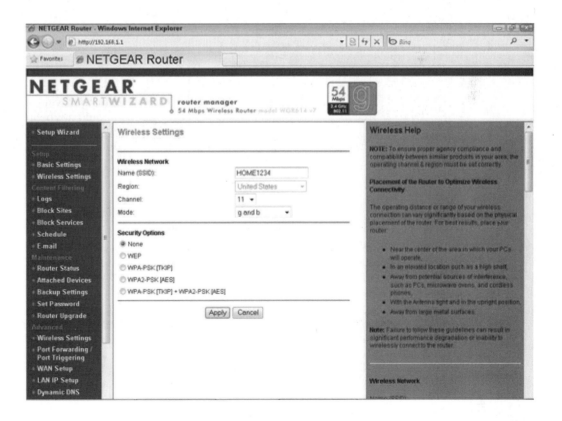

2. Under Wireless Network, enter a name (also known as an SSID) for your home network. Your SSID can be up to 32 characters in length and is case sensitive. For example, HOME1234 is not the same as *Home1234* because they use different case (capitalization).

Wireless Settings

Wireless Network

Name (SSID):	HOME1234
Region:	United States ▾
Channel:	11 ▾
Mode:	g and b ▾

Security Options

- ◉ None
- ○ WEP
- ○ WPA-PSK [TKIP]
- ○ WPA2-PSK [AES]
- ○ WPA-PSK [TKIP] + WPA2-PSK [AES]

[Apply] [Cancel]

3. Leave the Channel and Mode settings at their default values (most likely *11* and *g and b*, respectively). However, if you are installing multiple access points in your home with overlapping coverage — or your neighbors' wireless networks overlap your coverage area — and you are experiencing interference or poor signal strength, you can change your channel settings to one of the other options. The actual channel value does not matter. You just need to select one that minimizes interference with other access points. Changing your mode settings should not be necessary and will not have any effect on interference.

4. Under Security Options, select one of the available settings. For WEP, go to Step 5. For all others, go to Step 8.

Your SSID should be unique enough that you will know which wireless network is yours (it's likely that you will be able to detect your neighbors' SSIDs and vice versa), but not descriptive enough for others to identify you. For example, naming your wireless network *Apt2B* or *SmithFamily* is a bad idea (assuming you live in apartment 2B or your last name is Smith). This tells everyone which network they are trying to connect to and if someone is targeting you, they'll know exactly which network to steal data from.

I recommend choosing the strongest security option available on your wireless access point — WPA-PSK [TKIP] + WPA2-PSK [AES] in this example.

Wireless security protocols

Wireless networks are inherently insecure. Period. In the early days of wireless networking, manufacturers tried to make it as easy as possible for end users. The out-of-the-box configuration for most wireless networking equipment provided easy (pronounced "not secure") access to a wireless network.

Although many of these issues have since been addressed, the fact remains that wireless networks are generally not as secure as wired networks. Wired networks, at their most basic level, send data between two points, A and B, which are connected by a network cable. Wireless networks, on the other hand, broadcast data in every direction to every device that happens to be listening, within a limited range.

Various wireless security protocols were developed to protect wireless networks. These include WEP and WPA, along with several variations, each with their own strengths — and weaknesses. In addition to preventing uninvited guests from connecting to your wireless network, wireless security protocols encrypt your private data as it is being transmitted over the airwaves.

✔ **Wired Equivalent Privacy (WEP):** The original encryption protocol developed for wireless networks. As its name implies, WEP was designed to provide the same level of security as wired networks. However, WEP has many well-known security flaws, is difficult to configure, and is easily broken.

✔ **Wi-Fi Protected Access (WPA):** Introduced as an interim security enhancement over WEP while the 802.11i wireless security standard was being developed. Most current WPA implementations use a preshared key (PSK), commonly referred to as *WPA Personal*, and the Temporal Key Integrity Protocol (TKIP, pronounced *tee-kip*) for encryption. *WPA Enterprise* uses an authentication server to generate keys or certificates.

✔ **Wi-Fi Protected Access version 2 (WPA2):** Based on the 802.11i wireless security standard, which was finalized in 2004. The most significant enhancement to WPA2 over WPA is the use of the Advanced Encryption Standard (AES) for encryption. The security provided by AES is sufficient (and approved) for use by the U.S. government to encrypt information classified as top secret — it's probably good enough to protect your secrets as well!

Region:	United States ▼
Channel:	11 ▼
Mode:	g and b ▼

Security Options

○ None

◉ WEP (Wired Equivalent Privacy)

○ WPA-PSK [TKIP]

○ WPA2-PSK [AES]

○ WPA-PSK [TKIP] + WPA2-PSK [AES]

Security Encryption (WEP)

| Authentication Type: | Automatic ▼ |
| Encryption Strength: | 64bit ▼ |

Security Encryption (WEP) Key

| Passphrase: | WEPisBAD | [Generate] |

Key 1: ◉ `451784FFF6`

Key 2: ○ `CC4B3CD2C1`

Key 3: ○ `0E4BDC3E07`

Key 4: ○ `503923A4D2`

[Apply] [Cancel]

5. If you decide to set up WEP, select WEP under Security Options. Under Security Encryption (WEP), set the Authentication Type to Automatic and the Encryption Strength to either 64bit or 128bit. (128bit is better.) If you have network devices that fail to connect to your wireless network, you may need to set the Authentication Type to either Open System or Shared Key. This is sometimes necessary for older wireless cards or operating systems.

6. Under Security Encryption (WEP) Key, you can enter a passphrase and click the Generate button to automatically configure the WEP keys. If you chose 64bit encryption strength, four keys consisting of 10 hexadecimal digits (0-9, A-F) will be generated. If you chose 128bit encryption strength, one key consisting of 26 hexadecimal digits will be generated. Alternatively, you can manually enter a single hexadecimal key for WEP (10 hexadecimal digits for 64bit, 26 hexadecimal digits for 128bit).

7. Finally, click Apply.

TIP If configuring WEP seems overly complex, it is! Worse yet, you're only halfway there. Remembering your hexadecimal WEP key, configuring it on your PCs and other network devices, and actually getting them to successfully connect to your wireless network is enough to make you WEEP! And it's not even worth the effort! Choose one of the other security options (such as WPA-PSK [TKIP] or WPA2-PSK [AES]). They're exponentially more secure than WEP and exponentially easier to configure.

Wireless Settings

Wireless Network

Name (SSID): `HOME1234`

Region: `United States ▼`

Channel: `11 ▼`

Mode: `g and b ▼`

Security Options

○ None

○ WEP

○ WPA-PSK [TKIP]

○ WPA2-PSK [AES]

◉ WPA-PSK [TKIP] + WPA2-PSK [AES]

Security Options (WPA-PSK + WPA2-PSK)

Passphrase: `••••••••••`   (8-63 characters)

[Apply]   [Cancel]

8. If you decide to set up WPA-PSK [TKIP] or WPA2-PSK [AES] (or both), select the appropriate option under Security Options.

9. Enter a passphrase between 8 and 63 characters and click Apply. That's it!

Just because something is difficult, it isn't necessarily better. For example, configuring WEP is extremely complex, particularly compared to WPA or WPA2. But WEP security is more of a misnomer, and is in no way comparable to the strength of WPA and WPA2.

Configuring Your Wireless Network

Stuff You Need to Know

Toolbox:

- ✔ Computer
- ✔ Wireless access point (NETGEAR WGR614v7 in this example)

Time Needed:

10 minutes

You can configure your wireless access point to manage certain configuration information for the devices on your wireless network. For example, your wireless access point can automatically assign IP addresses, IP subnet masks, default gateway addresses, and DNS server addresses to all of your network devices using the Dynamic Host Configuration Protocol, or DHCP (see Chapter 2). This greatly simplifies the configuration and management of your home network.

1. Under Advanced on the left side of the window, click LAN IP Setup.

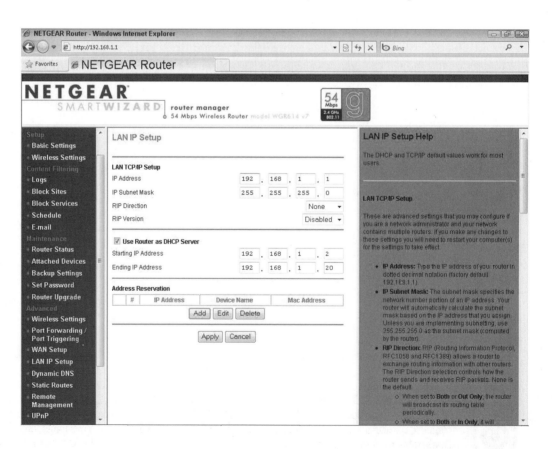

2. Under LAN TCP/IP Setup, either use the default settings for IP Address and IP Subnet Mask, or enter a different IP address and subnet mask. Leave RIP Direction and RIP Version set to their defaults (None and Disabled, respectively).

4. Enter an ending IP address within the same network range. You should allocate enough IP addresses to cover all the devices (for example, PCs and printers) on your network and a few extra for growth. For the most part, each device will require only one IP address. However, don't configure too many IP addresses. (The maximum is 254 in the example of a 192.168.1 network with host addresses from .1 to .254.) If an IP address is not available to be assigned to a device, it won't be able to connect to your wireless network. Thus, IP address management is one additional method to limit access to your network (albeit not a very secure method — DHCP is a first-come, first-serve protocol, so if your neighbor grabs the last available IP address on your network, you won't be able to connect to your own home network!). In this example, I've configured the ending IP address of 192.168.1.20 for a total of 20 host addresses (including the wireless access point).

3. In the next section, select the check box next to Use Router as DHCP Server. For the starting IP address, enter the next available host address in your IP address range. Recall that a subnet mask value of 255 indicates the network portion of your IP address, so every host on the network in this example will have a network IP address of 192.168.1. The host portion of the address is the number after the last decimal, so 2 would be the next available host address in this example. (Your wireless access point has host address 1, represented as 192.168.1.1.)

5. Click Apply to save your settings.

 IP addressing and subnet masks can be very difficult to understand. For the most part, you are limited to one of three private IP address ranges: 10.0.0.1–10.255.255.254, 172.16.0.1–172.31.255.254, and 192.168.0.1–192.168.255.254. I explain the difference between private and public IP addresses in Chapter 2. Unless you know what you are doing, you should strongly consider sticking with the default settings.

Connecting to Your Wireless Access Point

Stuff You Need to Know

Toolbox:

✔ Computer running Windows 7
✔ Wireless access point

Time Needed:

10 minutes

Now it's time to connect your computer to your wireless network. If you're connecting the computer you used to configure your wireless access point in the previous tasks, you can go ahead and disconnect the Ethernet network cable connecting your computer to your wireless access point. You're going wireless from here!

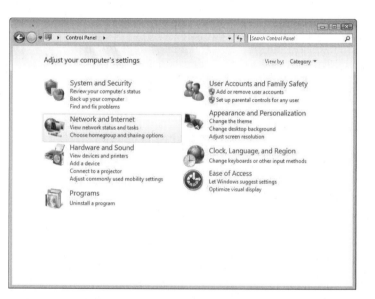

1. From the Control Panel, click Network and Internet.

2. Click Network and Sharing Center.

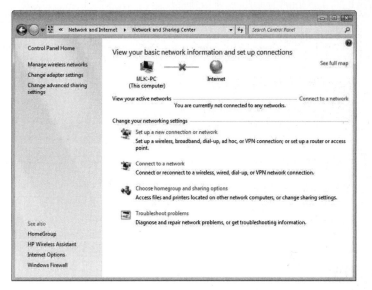

3. Click Connect to a Network.

4. On the pop-up screen in the lower-right corner of your screen, click your wireless network to expand it, and then click Connect.

5. Type your security key (the passphrase you previously created in the "Securing Your Wireless Access Point" task) in the Connect to a Network dialog box; you can optionally select the check box to hide characters for your security key.

6. Next, your computer connects to your wireless network.

7. Your computer is now connected! The Network and Sharing Center shows your active networks.

Setting Up an Ad Hoc Network

Stuff You Need to Know

Toolbox:
- ✔ Two computers with wireless cards
- ✔ Internet connection

Time Needed:
5 minutes

An alternative to installing a wireless access point is to set up a peer-to-peer (a network consisting of multiple desktop and laptop PCs, but no servers such as in a client-server network) ad hoc network. An *ad hoc network* provides basic wireless connectivity between two or more computers within 30 feet of each other. As the price of wireless access points has dropped, so too has the popularity of ad hoc networks. However, there are occasional situations where an ad hoc network provides all the wireless connectivity you need. For example, you may need to exchange files with a business associate at the airport (and don't have a USB thumb drive handy), or you may have a desktop PC connected directly to the Internet and want to share its Internet connection with your laptop. (See Chapter 8 to find out how to share an Internet connection.)

To configure an ad hoc network on a Windows 7 computer, follow these steps:

1. From the Control Panel, click Network and Internet.

2. Click Network and Sharing Center.

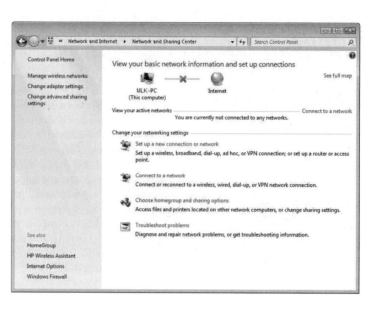

3. Click Set up a New Connection or Network.

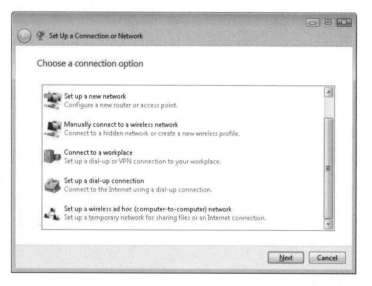

4. Scroll to the bottom of the menu options, select Set up a Wireless Ad Hoc (Computer-to-Computer) Network, and click Next.

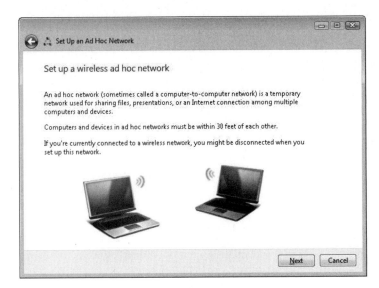

5. Click Next.

6. Enter a network name, choose a security type (the default is WPA2-Personal), and enter a security key (which is case-sensitive and 8–63 alphanumeric characters); you can optionally select the check boxes to hide characters for your security key and save this network for future use. Click Next.

I explain the different security types in the section "Securing your Wireless Access Point" earlier in this chapter.

7. Next, your ad hoc network is created.

8. Your ad hoc network is ready! A confirmation page shows your ad hoc network settings.

> Windows 7 has a quirk, a bug, dare I say — a security flaw. In Step 6, if you *select* the check box to hide characters in your security key, Windows 7 will show your network security key on the confirmation screen! If you leave the Hide Characters option *deselected* in Step 6, your network security key will be hidden on the confirmation screen! You should always be aware of curious eyes that may catch a glimpse of your security key when you're connecting an ad hoc network. It takes only a couple of minutes for a malicious person to connect to your ad hoc network and download your private files, and it's not uncommon for people to reuse passwords. So if you use your online banking password as your network security key (the key in the example above is *not* mine!), you may unwittingly compromise your banking accounts.

Part III
Setting Up Your Windows 7 Network

The 5th Wave — By Rich Tennant

"Oh, Arthur is very careful about security on the Web. He never goes online in the same room on consecutive days."

In this part . . .

Windows 7 has many rich features for home net-works. In this part, you find out how to set up user accounts, homegroups, file and print sharing, Internet connections, remote connectivity, PC gaming networks, and much more. It's time to start up your computer, turn the page, and start configuring your Windows 7 home network!

Chapter 5

Understanding User Accounts

User accounts make it possible for several people to use the same computer without affecting each other's personal settings or files, while maintaining accountability for their actions (who did what, and when). In this chapter, I explain why user accounts are important, the different types of user accounts in Windows 7, and how to perform important user account administration tasks.

Understanding User Profiles

A user profile stores an individual's customized settings and personal preferences. Additionally, a user profile maintains security for the individual's personal files, folders, e-mail, music, pictures, and more. Examples of settings that are maintained in a user profile include

✔ **Desktop preferences:** These include things such as your background color or a custom picture, screen saver, screen resolution, font size, shortcuts, icons, and folders, as well as how everything is arranged on your desktop.

✔ **Start menu options:** Different Start menu settings include what folders and programs are displayed, whether small or large icons are displayed, and how it's all arranged.

✔ **Internet settings:** These include your favorites (bookmarked Web sites), cookies, browser history, and cached Web pages.

It's possible to lose all of these settings and your personal files and folders in one fell swoop — by deleting an account. However, when deleting a user account, Windows 7 gives you the option of saving the user's profile. See the task "Deleting a User Account" later in this chapter for complete instructions.

Knowing the Difference in Administrator and Standard User Accounts

There are two types of user accounts in Windows 7 — Administrator and Standard User. To see whether an account is an Administrator or Standard User account, you can go to Manage Accounts in the Control Panel. (See Figure 5-1.)

The Guest account is a built-in Standard User account that does not require a password and provides only limited access to your network resources. I tell you more about the Guest account in the task "Turning the Guest Account On or Off" later in this chapter.

Figure 5-1: Administrator and Standard User accounts in Windows 7.

Administrator accounts have full permission to do just about everything in Windows, for example:

- ✔ Creating or deleting user accounts and changing passwords
- ✔ Changing or disabling security settings (such as parental controls, antivirus software, and Windows Firewall)
- ✔ Installing and removing software
- ✔ Viewing, changing, or deleting any user's files and folders

Thus, an Administrator account is often thought of as a power user account. Unfortunately, this has led to misuse of Administrator accounts over the years. *Power user* implies that someone is an advanced computer user and should therefore be entrusted with full access to everything on a computer or network. However, if you log in to an Administrator account every time you use your computer, regardless of whether you actually need to use administrator privileges during that particular session, you potentially open a security risk every time you log in to your computer or network. For example, if you are just surfing the Internet, you normally do not need administrator privileges. However, if you unknowingly browse to a malicious Web site that silently downloads spyware to your computer, the program will execute using the permission level of the logged-in user. Not all spyware requires administrator-level permissions to install and run itself on your computer, but it certainly makes it easier to infect your computer.

The other type of user account in Windows 7 is the Standard User. This should be the type of account you set up for most users on your network (including yourself). At least one Administrator account is required in Windows 7, but you shouldn't use it for your everyday computer access.

The downside of a Standard User account is that you may occasionally be inconvenienced if something you need to do actually does require administrator privileges — for example, installing or removing software. Fortunately, Windows 7 makes it relatively easy to perform administrator functions from a standard user account. If you are logged in as a standard user and attempt to do something that requires administrator-level permissions, Windows 7 prompts you to log in with an account that has the necessary permission level. If you know an Administrator account name and password, simply enter those credentials when prompted. Otherwise, someone with administrator permissions on your computer will need to enter the Administrator account credentials.

Administrator account passwords (or any passwords, for that matter) should not be shared with anyone and should be kept secret. If everyone knows the administrator password, anyone can wreak havoc on your computer. For example, your children may change the parental control settings to something a little more agreeable to them!

Creating a User Account and Password

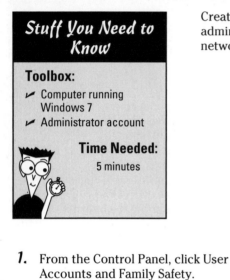

Stuff You Need to Know

Toolbox:
- Computer running Windows 7
- Administrator account

Time Needed:
5 minutes

Creating new user accounts and passwords is a basic network administration task. Follow these steps to set up the users on your network.

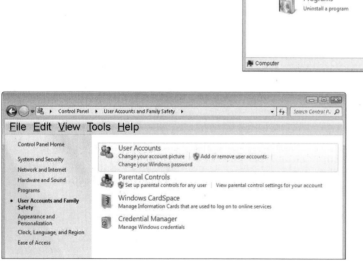

1. From the Control Panel, click User Accounts and Family Safety.

2. Under User Accounts, click Add or Remove User Accounts.

3. Below the list of user accounts, click Create a New Account.

4. Enter a name for the new user account and choose an account type. Click Create Account.

5. The new account is created and added to the list of user accounts. Click the user account that you just created.

6. Click Create a Password.

Creating better passwords

It's been said that a password is like a toothbrush: Use it regularly, change it often, and don't share it with anyone! These are good rules to remember, but you also need to have a good toothbrush . . . uhhh, password.

It's human nature to use passwords that are easily remembered (hence, easily guessed or broken). There are programs freely available on the Internet that can crack most passwords within a matter of minutes — even passwords that are complex (a mix of upper- and lowercase letters, numbers, and special characters such as an exclamation point or percent symbol). It's also human nature to use the same (or similar)

passwords across multiple accounts. So, while you may not be as concerned about the password on your home network, if it happens to be the same as the password on your corporate network or online banking account, you should be a little more concerned.

Despite these issues, passwords are by far the most common method for keeping computers, networks, and personal accounts (such as online banking and e-mail) safe today, and they are an inevitable fact of life for just about everyone who uses a computer. So with that in mind, here are a few guidelines for creating better passwords:

(continued)

(continued)

- Mix upper- and lowercase characters (for example, eXaMple)
- Replace some letters with numbers (for example, replace *e* with *3*)
- Combine two words by using a special character (for example, salt&pepper or bacon+eggs)

- Use the first letter from each word of a phrase, book title, or quote (for example, Home Networking Do-It-Yourself For Dummies becomes HNDIYFD)
- Use a combination of all the other tips in this list (for example, Snow White and The Seven Habits of Highly Effective People becomes SW+t7HoH3P)

7. Enter a new password for the user account and confirm the new password. You should also create a password hint to help you remember the password in case you forget it.

Create a password for Jackie's account

Jackie
Standard user

You are creating a password for Jackie.

If you do this, Jackie will lose all EFS-encrypted files, personal certificates and stored passwords for Web sites or network resources.

To avoid losing data in the future, ask Jackie to make a password reset floppy disk.

New password

Confirm new password

If the password contains capital letters, they must be typed the same way every time.
How to create a strong password

Type a password hint

The password hint will be visible to everyone who uses this computer.
What is a password hint?

Create password   Cancel

WARNING! The password hint will be visible to everyone. Although the hint should be helpful in remembering the password, it should not be a dead giveaway (for example, *Mom's maiden name* or *Make and model of my car*). Try something more subtle.

TIP From the Control Panel, you can go directly to the Manage Accounts menu by clicking Add or Remove User Accounts under User Accounts and Family Safety.

Changing or Removing Your Password

Stuff You Need to Know

Toolbox:

✔ Computer running Windows 7

Time Needed:
5 minutes

It is a good security practice to regularly change your password. Removing your password isn't such a good security practice, but it may be necessary from time to time!

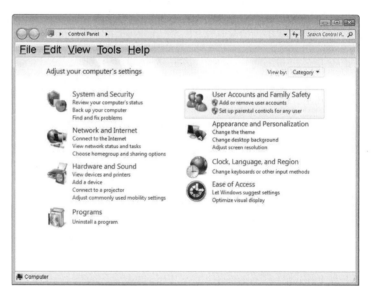

1. From the Control Panel, click User Accounts and Family Safety.

2. Under User Accounts, click Change Your Windows Password.

3. Under Make Changes to Your User Account, click Change Your Password (and go to Step 4) or Remove Your Password (and go to Step 5). Removing your password leaves your user account with no password — be careful if you choose this option because anyone can log into your account if they simply know your account name.

4. Enter your current password and your new password, and re-enter your new password to confirm. You should also enter a new password hint. Click Change Password.

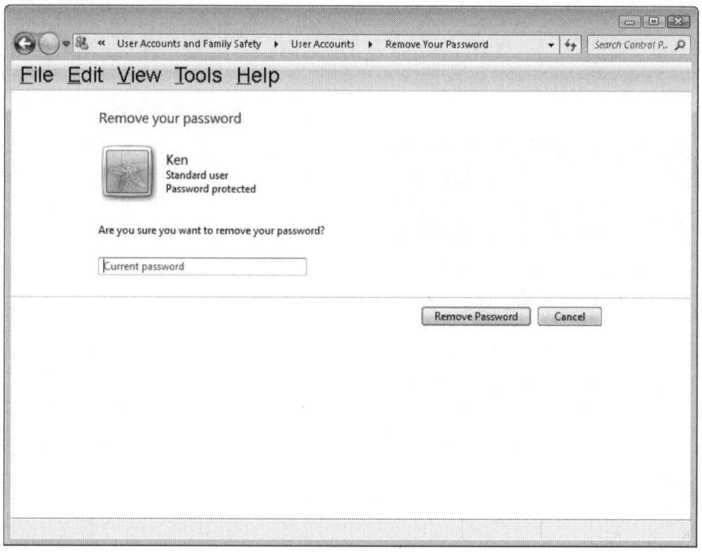

5. Enter your current password and click Remove Password.

Changing Your Account Picture

Stuff You Need to Know

Toolbox:
- Computer running Windows 7

Time Needed:
5 minutes

Windows 7 personalizes user accounts with a small picture that is associated with each account. It's kind of like picking what game piece you want in Monopoly. Fortunately, you've got a lot more choices than a car, dog, hat, shoe, iron, or thimble!

1. From the Control Panel, click User Accounts and Family Safety.

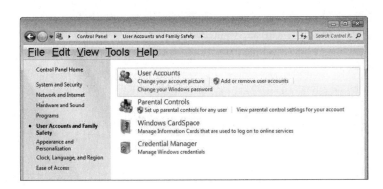

2. Click User Accounts.

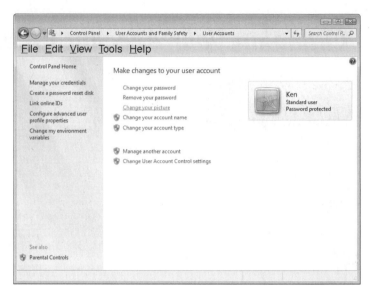

3. Under Make Changes to Your User Account, click Change Your Picture.

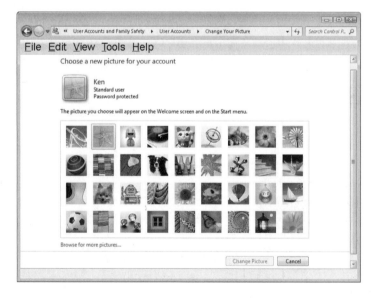

4. Choose a new picture. You can also browse for more pictures to import a personalized picture from your hard drive, network, or removable disk. Click Change Picture.

Renaming Your Account

Stuff You Need to Know

Toolbox:

✓ Computer running Windows 7

Time Needed:

5 minutes

If you decide to change the name of your account, you don't have to re-create it. Windows 7 makes it easy for you to simply rename your account.

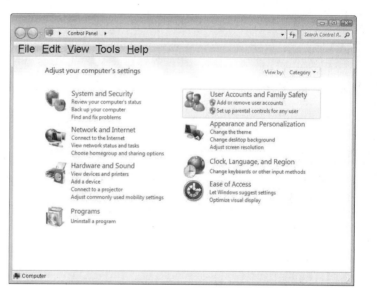

1. From the Control Panel, click User Accounts and Family Safety.

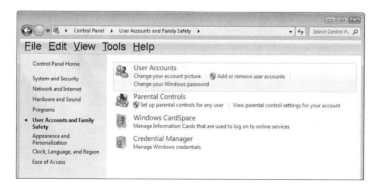

2. Click User Accounts.

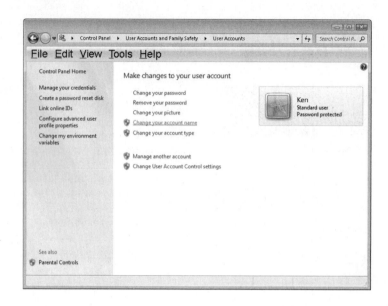

3. Under Make Changes to Your User Account, click Change Your Account Name.

4. Type in your new account name and click Change Name.

Deleting a User Account

Stuff You Need to Know

Toolbox:
- ✔ Computer running Windows 7
- ✔ Administrator account

Time Needed:
5 minutes

When an account is no longer needed, you can delete it from your computer or network. You cannot delete the account that you are currently logged in as, and you must be an administrator. Also, at least one Administrator account must remain (meaning you cannot delete the last Administrator account on the computer or network).

Warning: When you delete an account, it's permanent. Even if you recreate the account with the same name and password, Windows will treat it as a new account, and none of the settings from the previous account will exist in the new account. Of course, if you select Keep Files when deleting the account, you can manually copy those files and folders into the new account.

To permanently delete an account, follow these steps:

1. From the Control Panel, click User Accounts and Family Safety.

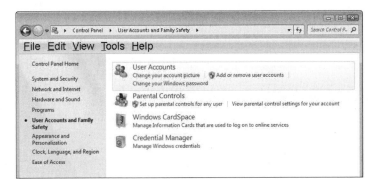

2. Under User Accounts, click Add or Remove User Accounts.

3. Click the user account that you want to delete.

4. Click Delete the Account.

5. Choose whether you want to save the account files. You can click Select Keep Files to save the user's desktop, Documents, Favorites, Music, Pictures, and Videos folders to a folder (with the user's name) on the current user's (Administrator) desktop — e-mail and other settings cannot be saved — or click Delete Files to delete the user account without saving any files, folders, or settings.

6. Confirm that you want to delete the user account by clicking Delete Account. Depending on your selection in the previous step, Windows will either indicate that you are deleting the user's account but keeping the user's files, or deleting the user's files and account.

Turning the Guest Account On or Off

Stuff You Need to Know

Toolbox:
- Computer running Windows 7
- Administrator account

Time Needed:
5 minutes

The Guest account is a built-in account that provides a convenient way for your visitors to have temporary access to your computer or network. Rather than setting up a separate account for your visitor, you can simply turn on the Guest account. The Guest account provides access to your computer or network (without a password), but no access to other people's files or settings. When your visitor leaves, you should turn the Guest account off (to keep any unwelcome visitors out).

To turn the Guest account on or off, follow these steps:

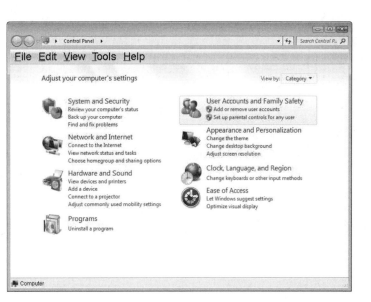

1. From the Control Panel, click User Accounts and Family Safety.

2. Under User Accounts, click Add or Remove User Accounts.

3. In the Manage Accounts window, click the Guest account.

4. Click Turn On to enable the Guest account.

5. To disable the Guest account, repeat Steps 1 through 3, and then click Turn Off the Guest Account.

To quickly turn the Guest account on or off, click the Windows 7 Start button, type **guest** in the search box, and then click Turn Guest Account On or Off. This takes you directly to the Manage Accounts window discussed earlier, in Step 3.

Creating a Password Reset Disk

Stuff You Need to Know

Toolbox:

✔ Computer running Windows 7

✔ CD-R, CD-RW, DVD-R, DVD-RW disc, or USB flash drive

Time Needed:
5 minutes

It occasionally happens. You find yourself floating in the open sea with bullet holes riddling your back and you can't remember anything! After watching *The Bourne Identity* a few times, you suspect that you may be a secret agent, and assassins are everywhere trying to kill you — but that's the least of your worries. You can't remember your password! How will you ever get access to your e-mail and personal files so that you can start piecing your life back together? Fortunately, Windows 7 has the solution: the password reset disk.

Warning: You can't create a password reset disk if you don't know your password, so don't wait for the day you actually need it. Go ahead and create it when you initially set up your user account. Remember, amnesia favors the prepared mind.

To create a password reset disk, follow these steps:

1. Insert a blank CD-R (or CD-RW) or DVD-R (or DVD-RW) disc into your computer's writeable CD (or DVD) drive, or a USB flash drive into one of your computer's USB ports.

2. From the Control Panel, click User Accounts and Family Safety.

3. Click User Accounts.

4. In the left task pane, click Create a Password Reset Disk.

5. The Forgotten Password Wizard appears. Click Next.

6. Select the drive where you want to create your password key disk — CD/DVD-RW or Removable Disk (USB).

7. Enter your current password, and then click Next.

8. Your password reset disk is created. Click Next.

9. Click Finish and store your password reset disk in a safe place (preferably somewhere that you won't forget).

You don't need to create a new password reset disk if you change your password. The password reset disk simply allows you to reset your password without losing your files and settings.

Using the Password Reset Disk

Stuff You Need to Know

Toolbox:
- Computer running Windows 7
- Password reset disk

Time Needed:
5 minutes

It's hopeless! You can't remember your password. Luckily, you created a password reset disk when you set up your account. Follow these easy steps and you'll be back in business in no time at all (well, maybe five minutes):

Tip: You don't have to update your password reset disk after using it to reset your password!

1. Turn your computer on. At the Windows login screen, leave the Password box empty and press Enter.

2. You will see a red *X* and a warning message that the username or password is incorrect. Click OK.

3. Insert your password recovery disk in the USB port or CD/DVD drive.

4. The login screen reappears with your password hint (if you set one up) below the Password box and a link to Reset Password below the hint. If the hint doesn't help you remember your password, click the Reset Password link.

5. The Password Reset Wizard appears. Click Next.

6. Select the drive location of your password reset disk from the drop-down menu (either the USB port or the CD/DVD drive). By default, the password reset file is not saved to a folder, so unless you created a folder and moved the file to that folder, simply select the drive location. Click Next.

7. Type a new password, confirm your new password, and enter a new password hint. Click Next.

8. Click Finish. Your password is reset.

9. Type your new password into the Password box to log in.

Chapter 6

Setting Up a HomeGroup

Tasks Performed in This Chapter

- ✔ Creating a homegroup
- ✔ Joining a homegroup
- ✔ Changing the homegroup password
- ✔ Changing sharing options
- ✔ Leaving a homegroup

Windows computers on a network have traditionally been organized by workgroups or domains.

A *Windows workgroup* is suited for only the smallest of networks (usually no more than 20 computers). A workgroup is considered a peer-to-peer network because there are typically no servers on the network. There is no password to protect the workgroup, so any computer can join the workgroup. Users must have an account on each computer in the workgroup to use that computer. You can share files and printers in a workgroup — but it isn't easy!

Windows domains, on the other hand, are found in small company networks consisting of only a dozen or so computers, as well as large multinational enterprises with thousands of computers. Windows domains scale extremely well, but can be very complex to manage. A Windows domain is considered a client-server network because servers centrally manage many functions, particularly security and permissions, across the entire domain. Users do not need to have individual accounts on each computer or server on the network that they want to use.

The *homegroup* is a new feature in Windows 7 that makes it easy for you to share documents, music, pictures, printers, and much more, with other Windows 7 computers on your home network. Like a Windows workgroup, it is considered a peer-to-peer network, and users must still have an account on each computer they want to use in the homegroup. However, a homegroup provides some security by requiring a password to initially join the homegroup, and a homegroup is far simpler to manage and share stuff across than either workgroups or domains.

Creating a HomeGroup

Stuff You Need to Know

Toolbox:
- Computer running Windows 7
- Administrator account

Time Needed:
5 minutes

The first thing you need to do when getting started with a homegroup is to create the homegroup! You can create a homegroup on any computer running Windows 7 Home Premium, Ultimate, Professional, or Enterprise edition.

Tip: If you're buying a new home computer or laptop with Windows 7 already installed, it most likely includes the Home Premium edition, but you should verify the edition before purchasing it. If it only includes the Starter or Home Basic edition, you should strongly consider an upgrade, unless you already have another computer running Windows 7 Home Premium (or higher). Netbooks typically include Windows 7 Starter or Home Basic edition.

Follow these steps to create a homegroup:

1. From the Control Panel, click Network and Internet.

2. Under HomeGroup, click Choose HomeGroup and Sharing Options.

3. Click Create a HomeGroup.

4. Select the items you would like to share with your homegroup. Click Next.

5. Windows will automatically generate a password for your homegroup. You need to write down or print this password because you will need it to join other computers to your homegroup. Click Finish.

Joining a HomeGroup

Stuff You Need to Know

Toolbox:
✔ Computer running Windows 7

Time Needed:
5 minutes

Any computer running any version of Windows 7 can join a homegroup. Follow these easy steps:

Warning: Only computers running Windows 7 can join a homegroup. There is no backwards compatibility with Windows XP or Vista, and Mac OS and Linux users can't join the party!

1. From the Control Panel, click Network and Internet.

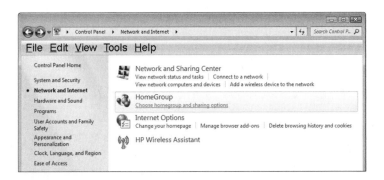

2. Under HomeGroup, click Choose HomeGroup and Sharing Options.

Share with other home computers running Windows 7

You have been invited to join a homegroup.

With a homegroup, you can share files and printers with other computers running Windows 7. You can also stream media to devices. The homegroup is protected with a password, and you'll always be able to choose what you share with the group.

Tell me more about homegroups

Change advanced sharing settings...

Start the HomeGroup troubleshooter

3. Click Join Now.

Share with other home computers running Windows 7

Windows detected a homegroup on your network. With a homegroup, you can share files and printers with other computers running Windows 7. You can also stream media to devices.

Tell me more about homegroups

Select what you want to share:

☑ Pictures   ☐ Documents

☑ Music   ☑ Printers

☑ Videos

4. Select the items you would like to share with your homegroup. Click Next.

Type the homegroup password

A password helps prevent unauthorized access to homegroup files and printers. You can get the password from the person who set up your homegroup.

Where can I find the homegroup password?

Type the password:

Gg6pP5ji52

5. Enter the password for the homegroup. Click Next.

If you don't know the homegroup password, go to another computer that is already a member of the homegroup and from the Control Panel, click Network and Internet, then click HomeGroup, and then under Other HomeGroup Actions, click View or Print the HomeGroup Password.

Changing the HomeGroup Password

Stuff You Need to Know

Toolbox:

- ✓ Computer running Windows 7
- ✓ Administrator account

Time Needed:

5 minutes

You may have noticed that the homegroup password that is automatically generated for you is a bit cryptic. Windows 7 does this because it's more secure than using a default password that everyone in the world will know (like *default* or *homegroup*). Also, Microsoft wanted to make it as easy as possible for you to set up a homegroup — just in case you're feeling creatively challenged when prompted for a homegroup password. And to reduce the possibility that you might reuse your own personal password for your homegroup, Windows 7 automatically generates one for you. If you'd like to change it to something else, follow these steps:

Tip: You need your homegroup password only to join a computer to the homegroup, so there's really no reason to change your homegroup password from the one that's automatically generated for you.

1. From the Control Panel, click Network and Internet.

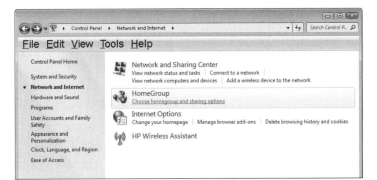

2. Under HomeGroup, click Choose HomeGroup and Sharing Options.

3. Under Other HomeGroup Actions, click Change the Password.

4. Click Change the Password.

5. You can type your own homegroup password, or click the refresh button to the right of the dialog box to have Windows 7 generate a new password. Click Next.

6. You will need to change the homegroup password on all of the other computers on your network for them to participate in your homegroup. Click Finish.

If you decide to change your homegroup password, you will need to change it on all the computers in your homegroup.

Changing Sharing Options

Stuff You Need to Know

Toolbox:

✔ Computer running Windows 7

Time Needed:
5 minutes

After creating or joining a homegroup, you might later change your mind about which libraries you want to share. Also, although the computer is a member of the homegroup, each individual user on the computer decides which of their libraries to share with the homegroup. Follow these steps to change your sharing options.

1. From the Control Panel, click Network and Internet.

2. Under HomeGroup, click Choose HomeGroup and Sharing Options.

3. Under Share Libraries and Printers, select the items (pictures, music, videos, documents, and printers) you would like to share. Deselect any you don't want to share. Click Save Changes.

Leaving a HomeGroup

Stuff You Need to Know

Toolbox:
- Computer running Windows 7

Time Needed:
5 minutes

Perhaps you've been voted off the island. Or you didn't get picked to be the quarterback, so you're taking your football and going home. For whatever reason, you've decided you no longer want to share with others and you don't want your computer to be a part of the homegroup.

Warning: If this is the computer the homegroup was created on, all computers that are joined to the homegroup will be disconnected.

Follow these steps to leave quietly:

1. From the Control Panel, click Network and Internet.

2. Under HomeGroup, click Choose HomeGroup and Sharing Options.

3. Click Leave the HomeGroup.

4. Verify you want to leave the homegroup by once again clicking Leave the HomeGroup.

5. The computer is disconnected from the home-group. Click Finish.

Chapter 7

Sharing With Others

Windows 7 provides three easy methods for sharing files and folders over your network: homegroups, Public folders, and manually sharing files, folders, disks, and devices. Homegroups are a nice new feature in Windows 7 that make it easy to share your files, folders, music, pictures, and videos with other people on your home network. Public folders let you share with others on your home network, including (welcome) guests that may not have their own username and password on your network. And, of course, you can still do things the old-fashioned way — manually, barefoot in the snow, uphill both ways — which may be your best option for sharing if you have computers on your home network that aren't running Windows 7 (such as Windows Vista or XP).

In this chapter, I show you how to share with others on your home network using all of the methods described here, as well as how to protect your files and folders with permissions and encryption, and how to access files and folders that others share with you.

Sharing in a HomeGroup

Stuff You Need to Know

Toolbox:
- ✔ Computer running Windows 7
- ✔ Home network
- ✔ Windows 7 HomeGroup

Time Needed:
5 minutes

The homegroup feature in Windows 7 was designed to make sharing as easy as possible. Through the homegroup, you can quickly and easily share folders, documents, pictures, music, videos, and printers. (To set up a homegroup in Windows 7, see Chapter 6 and then return here.)

1. From the Control Panel, click Network and Internet.

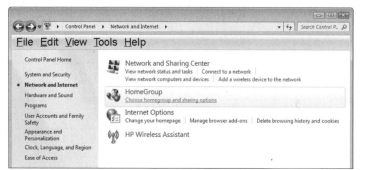

2. Under HomeGroup, click Choose HomeGroup and Sharing Options.

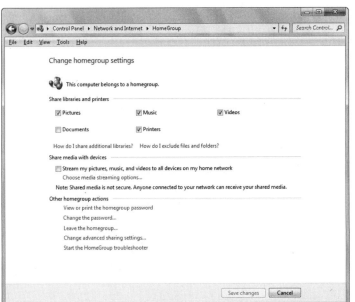

3. Under Share Libraries and Printers, select the items (pictures, music, videos, documents, and printers) you would like to share. Deselect any you don't want to share. Click Save Changes.

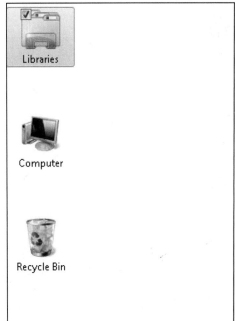

To share custom libraries or folders that you have created, follow these steps:

1. Click the Libraries icon on your desktop.

2. Select the custom library (or the custom folder within a library) that you would like to share (do not double-click it; just select it by clicking it once) and click Share With on the toolbar.

3. You can choose to share your custom library (or folder) with nobody, with your homegroup, or only with specific people. If you choose to share with your homegroup, you can allow the homegroup Read access, which allows others to open items within your custom library (such as documents, music, videos, or pictures) but not to make any changes to or add or delete anything in your custom library. Or you can allow Read/Write access, which allows others to also make changes to or add or delete anything in your custom library. If you wish to share only with specific people, click Specific People and continue to Step 4.

4. You can either type the username of the person you want to share with, or click the arrow to the right of the dialog box and select the person from the drop-down menu. Click Add.

5. The person is added with Read permission. To change the permission level, click the person you want to change permission for and select Read, Read/Write, or Remove (to remove file sharing for that person).

6. Click Share.

7. Windows asks if you want to give access to other people (the people you designated in the previous step). Click Next.

8. Windows confirms that your library is now shared. You can click the E-mail link to e-mail someone a link to your shared items, or the Copy link to copy and paste the link into a program. You can also click Show Me All the Network Shares on This Computer to open an Explorer window and directly access any shared network drives. Click Done.

Using Public Folders

Stuff You Need to Know

Toolbox:
✔ Computer running Windows 7

Time Needed:
5 minutes

Each Windows 7 library has a Public folder that allows you to quickly and easily share documents, pictures, videos, and music with anyone on your computer or network. Anyone with a user account on your computer or network can view, change, or delete files and folders in the Windows 7 Public folders, regardless of whether they have a Standard User or Administrator account.

1. To browse to the Public folders, double-click Libraries on your desktop. In the left pane, click the gray arrow to the left of Libraries, then click the gray arrow to the left of Documents, Music, Pictures, or Videos to expand the folder list and view the Public folders. You can drag and drop files or folders to the Public folders or browse to these folders when copying and pasting, or saving files.

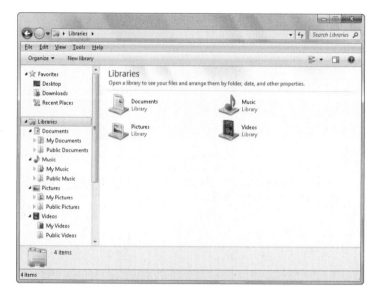

2. In order for others to access the Public folders on your computer, they will need to have their own user account on your computer. Each person using your network should have his own unique username and password, but that username and password should be the same on each computer on the network. This allows a user to log onto one computer and access the public folders on another computer on the network, without having to log in again on that computer.

WARNING!

Having the same username and password on all computers on your network is not without risk. If your username and password is discovered by a virus or malicious user on one computer, they will potentially be able to access your account on all computers on your network. You will have to decide whether the convenience of logging in only once is worth the tradeoff of some additional risk. Arguably, having a different username and password on each computer will slow you down more than it will a virus or attacker (because all of your usernames and passwords are likely to be variations of one username and password — it's human nature).

Turning Off and On Network Discovery

Stuff You Need to Know

Toolbox:
- Computer running Windows 7
- Home network
- Administrator account

Time Needed:
5 minutes

Network discovery helps computers on your network find each other easily. By default, network discovery is turned on. To change your network discovery settings, follow these steps:

Remember: Network discovery requires the following services to be running on your computer: DNS Client, Function Discovery Resource Publication, SSDP Discovery, and UPnP Device Host. Additionally, Windows Firewall (and any other firewalls on your network) must be configured to allow network discovery.

1. From the Control Panel, click Network and Internet.

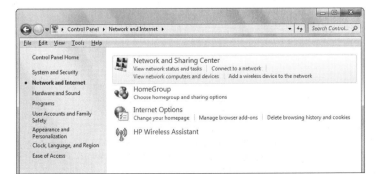

2. Click Network and Sharing Center.

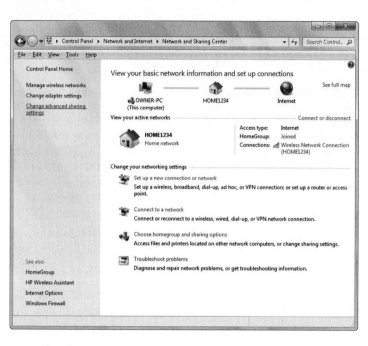

3. In the left pane, click Change Advanced Sharing Settings.

4. Windows creates separate network profiles for each of your networks (for example, Home or Work and Public. Under the current profile (or the profile you wish to change), scroll to the Network Discovery section and click Turn Off Network Discovery or Turn On Network Discovery (default). Click Save Changes.

Turning Off and On File and Printer Sharing

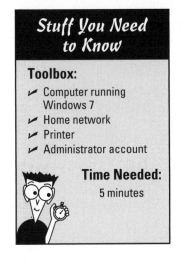

Stuff You Need to Know

Toolbox:
- ✓ Computer running Windows 7
- ✓ Home network
- ✓ Printer
- ✓ Administrator account

Time Needed:
5 minutes

On rare occasion, you may need to disable file and printer sharing (for example, if you are troubleshooting a network problem or trying to prevent a virus from spreading on your network). To turn file and printer sharing off or on, follow these steps:

1. From the Control Panel, click Network and Internet.

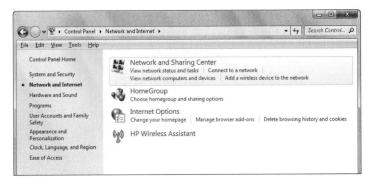

2. Click Network and Sharing Center.

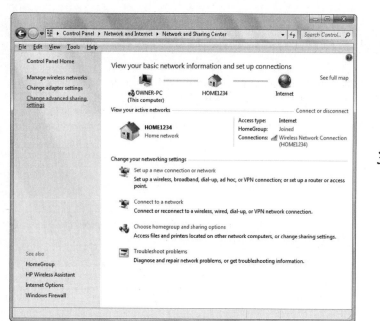

3. In the left pane, click Change Advanced Sharing Settings.

4. Windows creates separate network profiles for each of your networks (for example, Home or Work and Public). Under the current profile (or the profile you wish to change), scroll to the File and Printer Sharing section and click Turn Off File and Printer Sharing (or Turn On File and Printer Sharing). Click Save Changes.

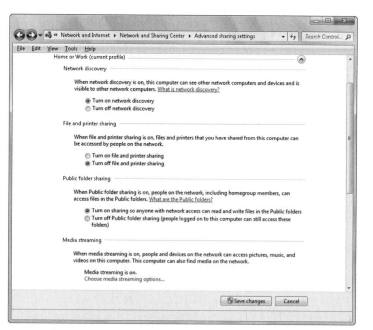

Turning Off and On Public Folder Sharing

Stuff You Need to Know

Toolbox:
- ✔ Computer running Windows 7
- ✔ Home network
- ✔ Administrator account

Time Needed:
5 minutes

To control whether Public folders can be accessed across your network, or only on the computer someone is logged into, follow these steps:

1. From the Control Panel, click Network and Internet.

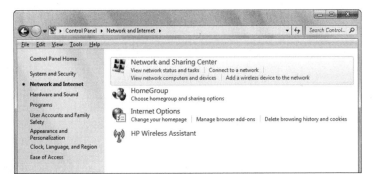

2. Click Network and Sharing Center.

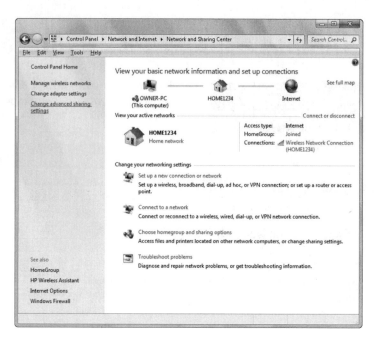

3. In the left pane, click Change Advanced Sharing Settings.

4. Windows creates separate network profiles for each of your networks (for example, Home or Work and Public. Under the current profile (or the profile you wish to change), scroll to the Public Folder Sharing section and click Turn Off Public Folder Sharing or Turn On Sharing (default). Click Save Changes.

Changing Media Streaming Options

Stuff You Need to Know

Toolbox:
- ✔ Computer running Windows 7
- ✔ Home network
- ✔ Administrator account

Time Needed:
5 minutes

You can easily share and stream media, such as music, pictures, TV programs, and videos across your network with Windows 7. To control what can be streamed across your network, follow these steps:

1. From the Control Panel, click Network and Internet.

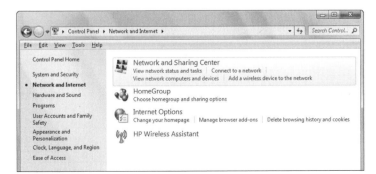

2. Click Network and Sharing Center.

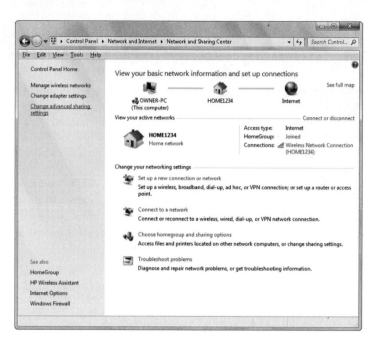

3. In the left pane, click Change Advanced Sharing Settings.

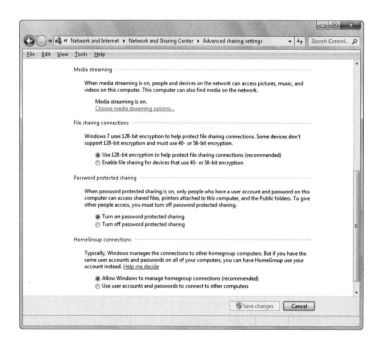

4. Windows creates separate network profiles for each of your networks (for example, Home or Work and Public). Under the current profile (or the profile you wish to change), scroll to the Media Streaming section and click Choose Media Streaming Options.

5. Enter a name for your media library. (The default is your account name.) Click Choose Default Settings.

6. In the Default Media Streaming Settings window, you can choose what Star and Parental ratings for music, pictures, recorded TV, and video that you want to allow to be streamed to other computers on your network. Make any desired changes and click OK.

7. You can override the default settings for all devices on your network by clicking the Allow All or Block All button above the list of devices. You can also select an individual device and choose Allowed or Blocked or click the Customize link.

8. If you click the Customize link, the Customize Media Streaming Settings window, (similar to the Default Media Streaming Settings window) appears. You can deselect the Use Default Settings check box and customize the media streaming options for the selected device. After you have made any desired changes, click OK.

By default, most of the items in your Windows Media Player library are automatically assigned a rating from 1 (lowest) to 5 (highest) stars. These ratings are assigned by third-party providers and online stores. You can manually change the rating by right-clicking the item you would like to change in Windows Media Player, selecting Rate from the drop-down menu, and clicking the new rating you would like to assign (1 to 5 stars, or unrated).

Changing File Encryption Settings

Stuff You Need to Know

Toolbox:

- Computer running Windows 7
- Home network
- Administrator account

Time Needed:
5 minutes

Typically, you want to use the strongest encryption available to protect the files on your network. However, if you have a device that does not support the maximum encryption setting in Windows 7 (128-bit), you may need to change the default setting to a lower encryption level (40- or 56-bit) in order to share files with that device.

1. From the Control Panel, click Network and Internet.

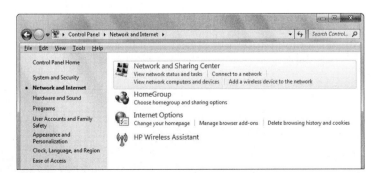

2. Click Network and Sharing Center.

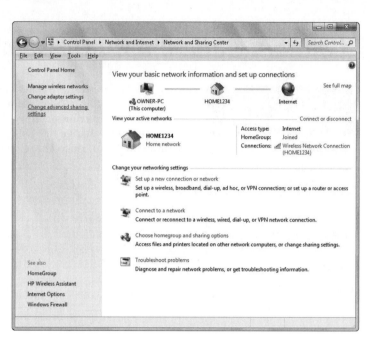

3. In the left pane, click Change Advanced Sharing Settings.

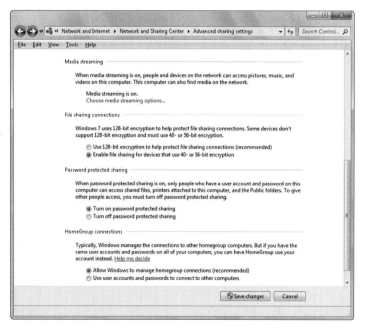

4. Windows creates separate network profiles for each of your networks (for example, Home or Work and Public. Under the current profile (or the profile you wish to change), scroll to the File Sharing Connections section and click Enable File Sharing for Devices That Use 40- or 56-bit Encryption or Use 128-bit Encryption (default). Click Save Changes.

Turning Off and On Password Protected Sharing

Stuff You Need to Know

Toolbox:
- Computer running Windows 7
- Home network
- Administrator account

Time Needed:
5 minutes

By default, a username and password is required to access files and folders across your network. However, you can easily disable this requirement (not recommended) by following these steps:

1. From the Control Panel, click Network and Internet.

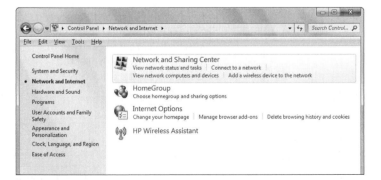

2. Click Network and Sharing Center.

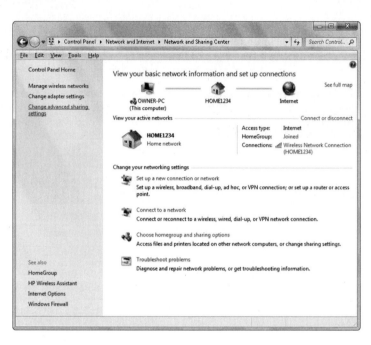

3. In the left pane, click Change Advanced Sharing Settings.

4. Windows creates separate network profiles for each of your networks (for example, Home or Work and Public). Under the current profile (or the profile you wish to change), scroll to the Password Protected Sharing section and click Turn Off Password Protected Sharing or Turn On Password Protected Sharing (default). Click Save Changes.

Changing HomeGroup Connection Settings

Stuff You Need to Know

Toolbox:

- ✔ Computer running Windows 7
- ✔ Home network
- ✔ Windows 7 HomeGroup
- ✔ Administrator account

Time Needed:
5 minutes

Letting Windows 7 manage your homegroup connections is the easiest way to share files and printers on your network. (To set up a homegroup in Windows 7, see Chapter 6 and then return here.) But if you have some computers on your network running Windows Vista, Windows XP, or even Mac OS — or if you just want to do things the old-fashioned way, using user accounts and passwords to connect across the network — follow these steps:

1. From the Control Panel, click Network and Internet.

2. Click Network and Sharing Center.

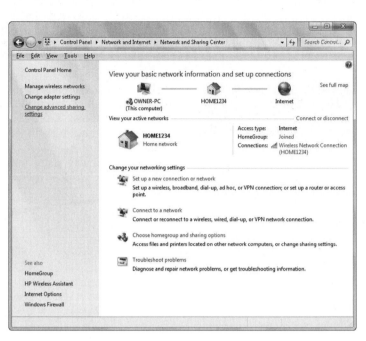

3. In the left pane, click Change Advanced Sharing Settings.

4. Windows creates separate network profiles for each of your networks (for example, Home or Work and Public). Under the current profile (or the profile you wish to change), scroll to the HomeGroup Connections section and click Use User Accounts and Passwords to Connect to Other Computers or Allow Windows to Manage HomeGroup Connections (default). Click Save Changes.

Sharing Other Files and Folders

In addition to your libraries, custom folders, and Public folders, you can share any folder on your computer.

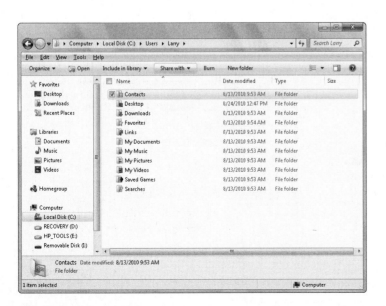

1. Open Windows Explorer by clicking Computer from your desktop and browse to the desired file or folder.

2. Select the desired file(s) or folder(s) and click Share With from the menu bar near the top of the Explorer window.

3. From the drop-down menu, select Nobody, HomeGroup (Read), HomeGroup (Read/Write), or Specific People.

4. If you choose Specific People, you can either type the username of the person you want to share with, or click the arrow to the right of the dialog box and select the person from the drop-down menu. Click Add.

5. The person is added with Read permission. To change the permission level, click the name of the person you want to change permission for, and select Read, Read/Write, or Remove (to remove file sharing for that person).

6. Click Share.

7. Windows confirms that your file(s) or folder(s) is now shared. You can click the E-mail link to launch your e-mail program, or the Copy link to copy the path to your network share(s) and let others know they now have access. Click Done.

When you share a folder, you also share all of the files and folders within that folder, unless you then change the permissions on the individual files or folders contained in the folder you just shared. The same permissions are also inherited by any new files or folders that you later create within that folder.

Sharing an Entire Disk

Stuff You Need to Know

Toolbox:
- Computer running Windows 7
- Administrator account

Time Needed:
10 minutes

If you don't need very granular control over who has access to the files and folders on your computer, you can easily share the entire disk. Sharing the entire disk means anyone you give access to can access anything on your computer. To share your entire disk, follow these steps:

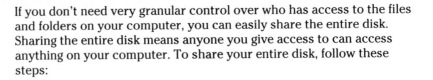

1. Open Windows Explorer by clicking Computer from your desktop and select the desired disk.

2. Right-click the selected disk, choose Share With, and then choose Advanced Sharing. The Local Disk Properties dialog box appears.

3. On the Sharing tab, under Advanced Sharing, click the Advanced Sharing button.

4. Select Share This Folder (but remember you're actually sharing the entire disk), and then give the share a name. (By default, it is the drive letter you are sharing.) You can also limit the number of simultaneous users that can connect to this disk. (The maximum is 20.) Next, click the Permissions button.

5. By default, Everyone is assigned Read permission. You can change the default permissions for the Everyone group by selecting the desired permissions (Full Control, Change, Read) under the Allow or Deny column. Windows will automatically select the appropriate check boxes to ensure you do not assign conflicting permissions for a user or group. (For example, you can't allow a user to have Change permission but deny that user Read permission.)

6. To add other users or groups, click the Add button.

7. Under Enter the Object Names to Select, type the account name of the person you would like to add, and click Check Names.

8. If the account name is found, Windows underlines your entry and also adds the name of the computer to the beginning of the account name. Click OK.

9. Select the added user's account name, and then modify the permissions as desired. (See Step 5.)

10. Click OK.

Accessing Shared Disks and Folders

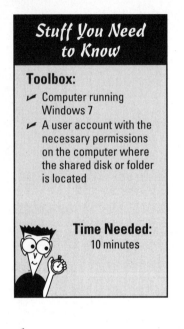

Stuff You Need to Know

Toolbox:
- Computer running Windows 7
- A user account with the necessary permissions on the computer where the shared disk or folder is located

Time Needed:
10 minutes

Once you've set up the files and folders you want to share, you need to know how to access those shared files and folders.

1. Open Windows Explorer by clicking Computer from your desktop. In the navigation pane on the left, you can click the small arrow to the left of Libraries, HomeGroup, Computer, or Network to expand the menu and access any shared files, folders, disks, or devices.

2. Double-click the object you would like to access. If prompted for a username and password, enter a username and password that has permission to access the object on the computer your are attempting to connect to.

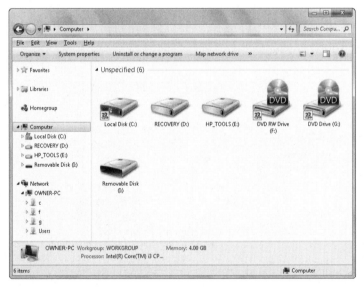

Accessing shared files and folders on your network from a Windows Vista or Windows XP computer is similar to the preceding steps. Just look for Network (Vista) or My Network Places (XP), browse to the shared location, and double-click.

Chapter 8

Connecting to the Internet

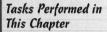

Sharing files and printers on your home network is fine, but connecting your home network to the Internet is where it gets exciting! Once your home network is connected to the Internet, you can access other networks practically anywhere in the world, play games, download music and videos, and much more!

In this chapter, I explain your different options for getting connected to the Internet and tell you how to connect your router or modem to your home network.

Choosing an Internet Service Provider (ISP)

Your choice of ISP (Internet service provider) is an important one. All too often, it is a love-hate relationship. You'll love all of your options, such as bundled packages that include your home and wireless phone service, and cable or satellite television, along with your high-speed Internet connection. You'll hate calling technical support when something goes wrong, and then waiting for the technician to show up at your house "sometime between noon and 4 p.m."

Unfortunately, ISPs are very rarely focused on customer service. They provide a service that people "can't live without" to a very large customer base. Oh, and they are very likely also your phone or cable provider, so they already have a reputation for outstanding customer service!

A few things you should consider when choosing an ISP include availability and convenience, speed, and cost. The two most common Internet options in most areas are high-speed broadband cable and DSL (digital subscriber line), which use your home cable television or telephone wiring, respectively. Less commonly, some areas may have high-speed wireless Internet service available. Other areas (particularly rural areas) may be limited to satellite or traditional dialup Internet service. Finally, cellular broadband (wireless) access is yet another, albeit relatively expensive, option for connecting to the Internet. See Table 8-1 for a comparison of the different types of Internet service.

Table 8-1	Comparing Internet Service Provider Options				
Type	Typical Download Speeds	Typical Upload Speeds	Approximate Monthly Cost	Advantages	Disadvantages
Cable	4–15 Mbps	384 Kbps– 1.5 Mbps	$40–$80	Very common, bundled packages, speed, reliability	Congested network may affect speeds
DSL	768 Kbps– 6 Mbps	128 Kbps– 768 Kbps	$15–$45	Very common, bundled packages, speed, reliability	Distance from telephone central office and old/faulty telephone wiring may affect speeds
Wireless	384 Kbps– 2 Mbps	Varies	$40–$60	Mobility	May require contract, may charge per data usage
Satellite	512 Kbps– 1.5 Mbps	128–256 Kbps	$50–$120	Available in rural areas	Poor reliability, high latency, setup costs
Dialup	56 Kbps	56 Kbps	$0–$20	Available almost anywhere	Ties up phone line, slow speed

Cable

Broadband cable Internet service provides high-speed, always-on access to the Internet. If you already have or are considering getting cable television service, it may be worthwhile to get cable Internet service as well. Your cable television company will usually offer a bundled Internet and cable television package (and possibly even digital phone service) that might save you some money. All that is required is a cable modem, which your cable television company will often provide free of charge. To install your cable modem, simply plug it into one of your cable television wall jacks using a coaxial cable (see Figure 8-1), just like the one used to connect your television. Then use an Ethernet cable to connect your cable modem to your computer or wireless router. (I tell you how to set up a wireless router in Chapter 3.)

Residential cable Internet download speeds are typically in the range of 4 to 6 Mbps. However, cable Internet service can be negatively impacted by the number of people in a neighborhood or area that simultaneously use the same cable Internet service. Also, cable service providers may limit the bandwidth available to individual customers to provide a relatively uniform level of service to an area (and so that they can charge a premium for higher speeds).

Figure 8-1: Coaxial cable used to connect a cable modem (or television).

Because your Internet cable service uses a different frequency than your cable television, you can surf the Internet and watch television at the same time without negatively affecting the signal quality of either.

DSL

If you don't have cable television service, you might be better served by DSL Internet access. However, if your home has old or faulty copper telephone wiring, DSL Internet service may not be your best option. DSL uses your existing telephone wiring, and all that is usually required is a DSL modem, which your phone company will often provide free of charge, along with a few line filters (which snap onto your phone lines to reduce interference). Installing a DSL modem is a relatively easy task, and a DSL modem (as opposed to a traditional modem) won't tie up your phone line while you're using the Internet. Your phone company will also likely offer some nice bundled packages, such as home and cellular phone service, and possibly satellite television, along with your Internet service.

DSL speeds are often advertised as a combination of two speeds: the download speed and the upload speed, such as 1.5 Mbps/384 Kbps. In this example, your download speed would be 1.5 megabits per second, and your upload speed would be 384 kilobits per second. Generally, your download speed is far more important because you download far more data than you upload. For example, when you go to a Web page by typing in the Web address (such as www.microsoft.com), you are uploading data (a Web site address). The relative size of that upload is very small compared to all of the graphics and content that is downloaded (as Microsoft's Web page) to your computer.

The speed of a DSL connection can be negatively impacted by factors such as the quality of the phone line (or age of the copper wiring) in your home, and the distance between your home and the phone company's central office (as this distance increases, speed decreases).

In theory, cable is faster than DSL, but in reality, the speeds are often comparable.

Wireless (cellular)

Wireless Internet service providers (WISPs) deliver Internet connectivity over radio waves rather than traditional wired infrastructure (such as cable or DSL) at speeds typically ranging from 384 Kbps to 2 Mbps. The types of WISPs include these two:

✓ **Nationwide:** Large (often global) providers such as T-Mobile, Clearwire, and Boingo that provide roaming Internet access via hot spots in large metropolitan areas, airports, hotels, and other popular locations.

✓ **Local:** Smaller companies that provide Internet access in isolated or rural areas where other high-speed options such as cable or DSL are typically not available.

Connecting to a nationwide WISP requires a wireless adapter, a wireless plan or contract, and software from your WISP to help you locate hot spot locations. Setting up an Internet connection with a local WISP typically requires a wireless modem or repeater provided by the WISP. Like any wireless device, it may be necessary to try placing the wireless modem in different areas throughout your home to find the best signal.

Do not confuse wireless Internet service with a wireless network. Although they both use the same technology and equipment, a wireless network by itself does not provide Internet access. You need an ISP to surf the Web!

Satellite

Satellite Internet service may be an option if you live in a rural area that doesn't offer cable or DSL. Generally, satellite service is more expensive and less reliable than other Internet options, and may require a long-term (one- or two-year contract). Also, because of transmission delays over long distances (sending Internet traffic from terra firma to outer space and back again), certain applications such as Skype or Vonage (Voice over IP, or VoIP) and virtual private network (VPN) connections (see Chapter 9) may not work well.

Dialup

Yet another option is to use traditional dialup Internet service. Most computers sold today have a built-in dialup modem (although this may go the way of floppy drives in a few years — that is, away!). Dialup phone service is usually less expensive than any of the other Internet options, but the savings are rarely worth the tradeoff in speed and convenience. A dialup modem is limited to 56 Kbps (that's *kilobits* per second!) and ties up your phone line while you're surfing the Internet. (Remember those annoying screeching sounds? No, not your ex!) Dialup Internet connections are painfully slow, and sharing a dialup connection across your home network isn't practical. Still, if you opt to use a dialup Internet service, make sure your ISP provides toll-free numbers for you to connect with, and consider adding a second phone line if you plan to spend any significant amount of time on the Internet but still need to make and receive home phone calls.

Installing Your Cable Modem or DSL Router

Your ISP will most likely provide all of the equipment and instructions you'll need to quickly and easily get started surfing the Internet! But in case you lost the instructions in all your excitement — or your ISP forgot to pack the instructions for whatever reason — here's an overview of the steps necessary to install your new modem or router:

1. Connect your cable modem to your wall cable television jack using a coaxial cable or connect your DSL router to your wall phone jack using a telephone cable. If you are using DSL, snap line filters (usually supplied by your DSL service provider) on any of your other phone lines to reduce interference.

2. Connect the Ethernet port of your cable modem or DSL router to an Ethernet port on your computer, network switch, or wireless access point (or wireless router) using an Ethernet network cable. (See Chapters 3 and 4.)

3. Turn on your cable modem or DSL router and wait about two minutes. This gives your modem enough time to boot up and establish a connection to the Internet.

WARNING!

Your computer will likely have a built-in dialup modem with a phone port. Do not confuse the phone port with your Ethernet port. If your Ethernet cable doesn't fit the port, you've got the wrong port. Keep looking!

Chapter 9

Connecting Remotely

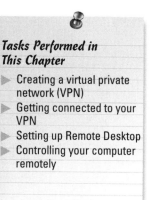

Tasks Performed in This Chapter

▶ Creating a virtual private network (VPN)

▶ Getting connected to your VPN

▶ Setting up Remote Desktop

▶ Controlling your computer remotely

If you find yourself basking on an exotic beach in some remote corner of the world and suddenly feeling homesick and anxious about leaving your home network home alone, take a deep breath, order another fruity drink with a paper umbrella, and relax! Windows 7 brings your home network to you — practically anywhere!

In this chapter, I show you how to connect to your home network over a secure Internet connection (VPN) and log into your computer using Remote Desktop.

Understanding Virtual Private Networks (VPNs)

A *virtual private network* (VPN) creates an encrypted tunnel between two computers or networks across the Internet. It makes communicating over the Internet as secure as if you were communicating from one room to another in the safety of your own home.

There are many complex security protocols used to establish a VPN connection, and there are also different types of VPN connections. Fortunately, setting up a VPN in Windows 7 is relatively easy and doesn't require you to be a cryptographic expert or mathematical genius!

Many companies allow their employees to connect to the corporate network from outside the office using a VPN. Although it's possible to use the Windows 7 VPN client, most companies use a third-party VPN client (such as a Cisco, Nortel, or SonicWALL VPN client) to connect through a corporate firewall. Alternatively, many companies use SSL (Secure Sockets Layer) VPNs to provide secure, but relatively limited, access to the company network using a Web browser (such as Internet Explorer or Mozilla Firefox).

Setting Up a Virtual Private Network (VPN) on Your Home Network

Stuff You Need to Know

Toolbox:

✔ Computer running Windows 7

Time Needed:
5 minutes

Follow these steps to set up a VPN on your home network so that other computers and devices can connect securely over the Internet:

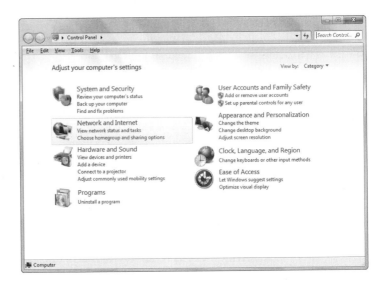

1. From the Control Panel, click Network and Internet.

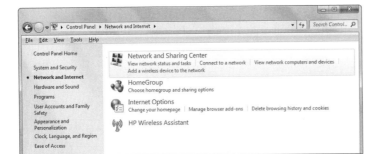

2. Click Network and Sharing Center.

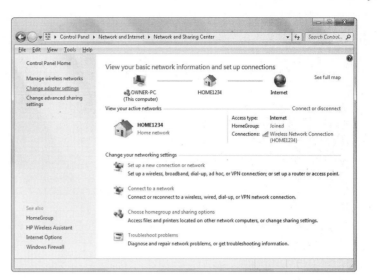

3. In the left pane, click Change Adapter Settings.

4. In the menu bar, click File, and then click New Incoming Connection.

5. In the Allow Connections to This Computer Wizard, select the user or users that you would like to set up for remote access. Click Next.

6. Under How Will People Connect?, select Through the Internet. If you have a dialup modem configured on your computer, you can also select Through a Dial-Up Modem. Click Next.

7. Under Networking Software, you can select the services to be enabled over your remote connection and install additional software or services. By default, Internet Protocol Version 4 (TCP/IPv4), File and Printer Sharing for Microsoft Networks, and QoS Packet Scheduler are selected. Click Allow Access.

If the user you would like to set up for remote access doesn't have an account on your computer, you can quickly create a new account by clicking the Add Someone button.

If you will be using a dialup connection for remote access, you can configure callback security by clicking the Account Properties button, and then clicking the Callback tab. With callback security, you can configure your computer to hang up after answering a remote call, and then either call back a specified number (such as your office number) or allow the caller to specify a callback number (less secure). By default, callback is not allowed.

Under Internet Protocol Version 4 (TCP/IPv4), you can change the properties to allow or prevent callers from accessing your network. You can also choose between allowing your network to assign an IP address to remote computers using DHCP (the default; see Chapter 2), statically assign an IP address, or allow the remote computer to specify its own IP address. File and Printer Sharing for Microsoft Networks allows remote computers to access shared files and printers on your network, and QoS Packet Scheduler prioritizes certain network traffic to improve the quality of the connection.

8. Windows configures your remote connections.

9. Once configured, Windows provides the computer name for the connection. *Note:* Although Windows says you will need to know this name in order to connect to your computer remotely, you can't actually use this name. Instead, you'll need the public IP address of the computer. (See Chapter 2 to learn about IP addresses.)

Setting Up a Remote Computer to Connect to Your Home Network

Stuff You Need to Know

Toolbox:
- Computer running Windows 7

Time Needed:
5 minutes

Once you've set up a VPN on your home network, you need to set up the devices that will remotely connect to your home network, such as a laptop.

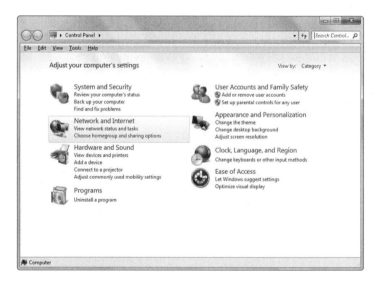

1. From the Control Panel, click Network and Internet.

2. Click Network and Sharing Center.

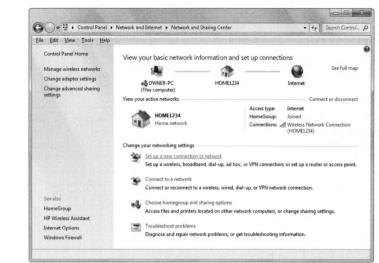

3. Under Change Your Networking Settings, click Set up a New Connection or Network.

4. Click Connect to a Workplace. Click Next.

5. Click Use My Internet Connection (VPN).

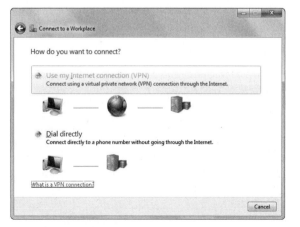

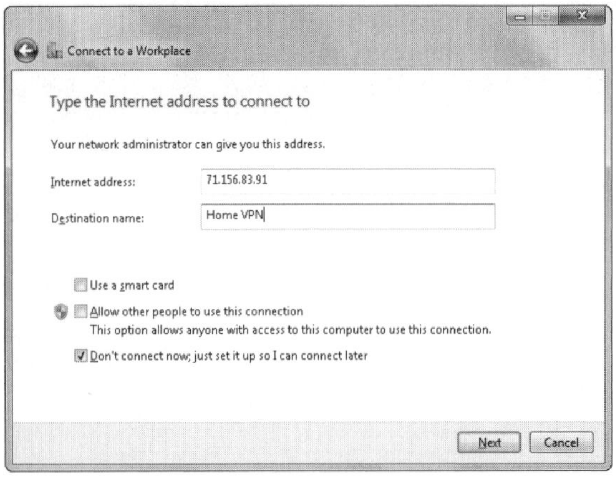

Type the Internet address to connect to

Your network administrator can give you this address.

Internet address: 71.156.83.91

Destination name: Home VPN

☐ Use a smart card

☐ Allow other people to use this connection
    This option allows anyone with access to this computer to use this connection.

☑ Don't connect now; just set it up so I can connect later

Next   Cancel

6. Enter the public IP address (see Chapter 2 to learn about public IP addresses) for the computer you are connecting to and a name for your VPN connection. Select Don't Connect Now; Just Set It up so I Can Connect Later. Click Next.

7. Enter your username and password for the computer or network you will be connecting to. Select Remember This Password if you want to automatically log in when you connect to your remote network using a VPN connection.

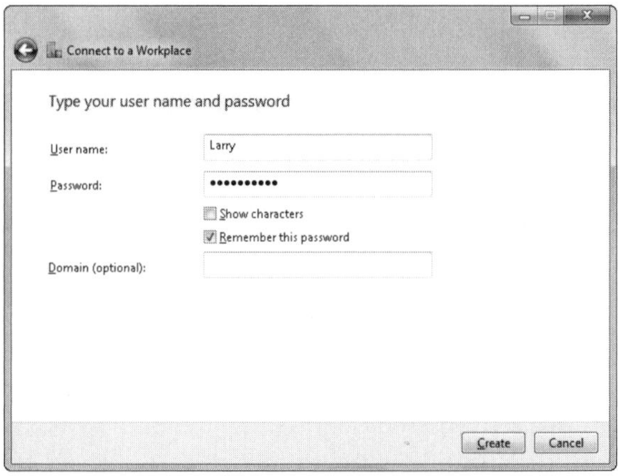

Type your user name and password

User name: Larry

Password: ●●●●●●●●●●

☐ Show characters
☑ Remember this password

Domain (optional):

Create   Cancel

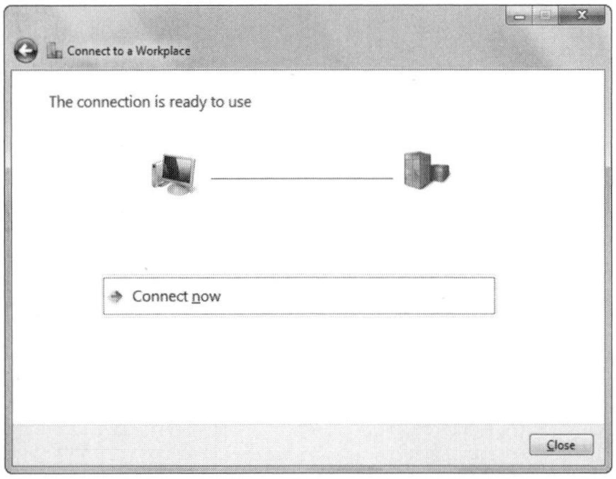

The connection is ready to use

→ Connect now

Close

8. Your VPN connection is now set up.

Connecting to Your Home Network over a VPN

Stuff You Need to Know

Toolbox:

- Computer running Windows 7
- Internet connection

Time Needed:
5 minutes

Now that both ends of your VPN connection are set up, it's time to get connected!

Warning: Additional configuration may be necessary on your router or firewall in order to successfully connect two computers over a VPN. For example, you may have to configure port forwarding on your router or permit certain types of traffic across your firewall. Refer to your router or firewall documentation for specific instructions.

1. From the Control Panel, click Network and Internet.

2. Click Network and Sharing Center.

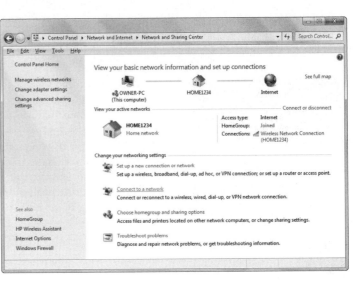

3. Under Change Your Networking Settings, click Connect to a Network.

4. In the pop-up window that appears, click your VPN connection, and then click Connect.

5. If you haven't saved your username and password, or you need to change your username and password, enter them here and click Connect. Otherwise, just click Connect.

6. To disconnect from your VPN, repeat Steps 1 through 4, and then click Disconnect.

Setting up Remote Desktop

Stuff You Need to Know

Toolbox:

- ✔ Computer running Windows 7

Time Needed:
5 minutes

A VPN allows you to connect to your home network securely over the Internet to access files and resources, such as printers. But a VPN also makes it possible for you to securely connect to your computer and *control* it remotely using software such as Remote Desktop — which is conveniently included with Windows 7!

Tip: There are also lots of third-party remote access/remote control programs available on the Internet at little or no cost. Examples include GoToMyPC (www.gotomypc.com), LogMeIn (www.logmein.com), and a variety of flavors of *VNC* (virtual network computing; for example, www.realvnc.com, www.tightvnc.com, and www.ultravnc.com).

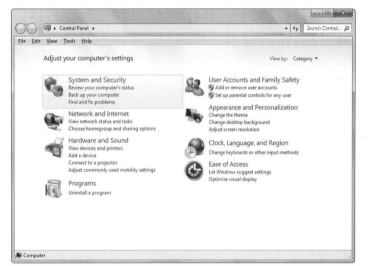

1. From the Control Panel, click System and Security.

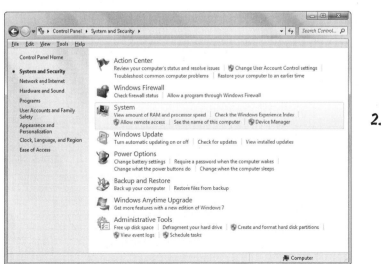

2. Click System.

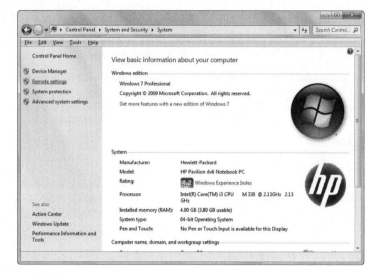

3. In the left pane, click Remote Settings.

4. From the Remote tab, select Allow Connections Only from Computers Running Remote Desktop with Network Level Authentication (More Secure). If you will be connecting to this computer using a version of Windows other than Windows 7 (for example, Windows XP or Windows 2003), select Allow Connections from Computers Running Any Version of Remote Desktop (Less Secure). Click Select Users.

5. In the Remote Desktop Users dialog box, click Add.

Select Users

Select this object type:

Users or Built-in security principals   [Object Types...]

From this location:

OWNER-PC   [Locations...]

Enter the object names to select (examples):

Larry   [Check Names]

[Advanced...]   [OK]   [Cancel]

6. In the Select Users dialog box, type the usernames of anyone you want to allow access to your computer via Remote Desktop. Click the Check Names button to verify that the account names exist on your computer, and then click OK.

Remote Desktop Users

The users listed below can connect to this computer, and any members of the Administrators group can connect even if they are not listed.

Larry

Ken already has access.

[Add...]   [Remove]

To create new user accounts or add users to other groups, go to Control Panel and open User Accounts.

[OK]   [Cancel]

7. Click OK.

System Properties

Computer Name | Hardware | Advanced | System Protection | Remote

Remote Assistance

☑ Allow Remote Assistance connections to this computer

What happens when I enable Remote Assistance?

[Advanced...]

Remote Desktop

Click an option, and then specify who can connect, if needed.

○ Don't allow connections to this computer

○ Allow connections from computers running any version of Remote Desktop (less secure)

● Allow connections only from computers running Remote Desktop with Network Level Authentication (more secure)

Help me choose   [Select Users...]

[OK]   [Cancel]   [Apply]

8. Click OK again.

Using Remote Desktop

Stuff You Need to Know

Toolbox:
- ✔ Computer running Windows 7
- ✔ Internet connection

Time Needed:
5 minutes

Remote Desktop (and other remote control software) makes working remotely *look and feel* just like you're sitting in front of your computer at home.

1. From the Start menu, choose All Programs, Accessories, Remote Desktop Connection.

2. Type the public IP address of the computer you wish to connect to, and click Connect. If you have used Remote Desktop to connect to a computer before, the computer name or IP address will appear in the drop-down list. When prompted, enter your username and password.

3. Your computer will now connect to the remote computer using Remote Desktop. The Remote Desktop screen will look exactly like a Windows desktop and works exactly the same way. Click an icon on the desktop or the Start button in the lower left corner to get going!

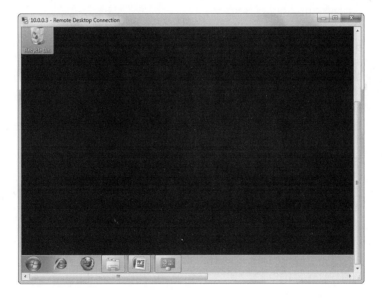

Customizing Remote Desktop

Stuff You Need to Know

Toolbox:
- Computer running Windows 7
- Internet connection

Time Needed:
5 minutes

Remote Desktop (and other remote control software) makes working remotely *look and feel* just like you're sitting in front of your computer at home.

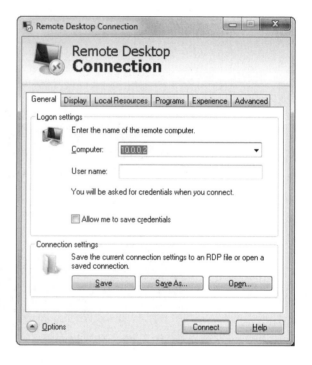

1. From the Start menu, choose All Programs, Accessories, Remote Desktop Connection.

2. Type the public IP address of the remote computer connection you wish to customize and click Options in the lower-left corner of the Remote Desktop Connection window. Under the General tab, you can enter your username and save your credentials. You can also save your connection settings.

3. Under the Display tab, you can resize the desktop display and change the color resolution.

4. Under the Local Resources tab, you can configure remote audio settings (play and record
audio from the remote computer), configure the
remote keyboard, and choose devices and
resources (such as printers and the clipboard)
that you want to use on the remote computer.

5. Under the Programs tab, you can configure certain programs to automatically start when you
connect to a Remote Desktop session.

6. Under the Experience tab, you can select your network or Internet connection speed to optimize the performance of your Remote Desktop session, enable or disable certain Windows desktop settings, and enable automatic reconnection if your Remote Desktop session is dropped.

7. Under the Advanced tab, you can configure Server authentication options, and configure Remote Desktop Gateway settings for better security of your remote sessions.

8. Under the General tab, click Save or Save As under Connection Settings to save your customized Remote Desktop settings.

If you connect to a VPN before establishing a Remote Desktop session, all of your network traffic will be encrypted and you can connect to your computers remotely using their computer name or private IP address (instead of having to use a public IP address).

Chapter 10

Having Fun with Your Home Network

Tasks Performed in This Chapter

- ✔ Connecting a gaming console to your home network
- ✔ Going hardcore with a gaming PC
- ✔ Building the home of the future
- ✔ Networking your home security system

All work and no play makes Jack a dull boy, right? In this chapter, I tell you about some of the really cool (and fun) things you can do with your home network.

Networking Your PlayStation, Wii, or Xbox 360

Since the early days of the Internet, online PC gaming has been hugely popular. Of course, there's no way that the big three (I'm talking about Nintendo, Microsoft, and Sony — not General Motors, Ford, and Chrysler) are going to miss out on this action! Connecting your gaming console to your home network and a broadband Internet connection is a great way to take your gaming prowess to the next level — or the next 30 levels, for that matter! And doing so brings you more than just games. Gaming consoles can be used for Web surfing, e-mail, movie watching, and more. Additionally, a network connection allows you to download and install *firmware* (system software) upgrades for your console, keeping it up to date and adding the latest and greatest features to the console.

Don't even bother setting up your gaming console for online gaming if you don't have a broadband Internet connection. If you think dialup Internet is painfully slow downloading e-mails, wait until you try online gaming! Spare yourself the misery and headaches — go with a broadband Internet connection. In fact, many games (and some of the gaming consoles) *require* a broadband Internet connection to play online.

Connecting your gaming console to a wireless home network is relatively simple. The Nintendo Wii and Sony PlayStation 3 have built-in Wi-Fi networking capabilities. (Note that a few of the earliest PlayStation 3 models — the 20GB models — did not include Wi-Fi, but the vast majority out there and all being sold now do.) All but the newest version of the Microsoft Xbox 360 require an Xbox 360 Wireless N Networking Adapter ($100; www.xbox.com/en-us/xbox360/accessories/cablesnetworking/home). If you have the latest and greatest Xbox 360 console, it has built-in 802.11n wireless networking. The Sony PlayStation 2 and original Microsoft Xbox both have built-in Ethernet ports for a wired network connection, but you'll need to buy specialized wireless adapters to connect either of these systems to a wireless network.

If you have an older-generation gaming console, you may need to purchase a Wi-Fi Ethernet bridge to connect it to your wireless home network. A *bridge* simply bridges the connection between a device's Ethernet port and a wireless access point. You don't need to install any special software or configure anything differently on your gaming console because Wi-Fi Ethernet bridges are plug and play. If you have encryption (such as WPA) set up on your wireless network, you'll need to plug your bridge into a wired connection first to enter the security settings in order for it to access your wireless home network. Just follow the installation wizard or quick setup instructions that are included with your Wi-Fi Ethernet bridge.

If you do not have encryption set up on your wireless home network, go to Chapter 4 — go directly to Chapter 4; do not pass Go; do not collect $200!

Two examples of Wi-Fi Ethernet bridges are the D-Link DGL-3420 Wireless 108AG Gaming Adapter (`www.dlink.com`; approximately $100) and the SMC SMCWEBT-G EZ Connect g Wireless Ethernet Bridge (`www.smc.com`; approximately $80).

Not all Wi-Fi Ethernet bridges support WPA encryption. If you're using WPA on your wireless home network (which I highly recommend), make sure you choose a Wi-Fi Ethernet bridge that supports WPA.

Since all of the current-generation gaming consoles have been on the market for three or more years, my focus in this chapter is connecting them to your home network rather than spending time on outdated gaming consoles. However, if you've got one of these older consoles, know that you *can* connect it to your network with the appropriate hardware (Wi-Fi Ethernet bridges, for example).

If you happen to have a wired Ethernet connection (CAT 5e or CAT 6 cable running into a wall outlet where you're setting up your console), you can skip the wireless connection we talk about here and just plug the console into the network with an Ethernet patch cable. Just follow the instructions for setting up a wireless connection discussed at the end of this chapter, choosing the "wired" instead of "wireless" option. *Note:* If your console is a Nintendo Wii, you'll have to buy Nintendo's Wii LAN Adapter ($24.95 on the Nintendo online store) and plug that into a USB port on your Wii to make an Ethernet connection.

Online Gaming Services for Gaming Consoles

Once you've connected your gaming console to your network (see the appropriate task for your gaming console later in this chapter), it's time sign up for an online gaming service. Sony, Nintendo, and Microsoft all offer online gaming services that enable head-to-head Internet game play, game downloads, chat, shopping, and Web browsing.

There are practically hundreds of PlayStation, Wii, and Xbox console games built for online playing, but not all games are online capable. Be sure to check the online capabilities of your individual games before attempting to play one online! If a game supports online play, it's clearly marked on the box or in online reviews and descriptions.

PlayStation Network

The *PlayStation Network* is a free service for Sony PS3 and PSP (PlayStation Portable) gamers that provides exclusive content including games, movies, videos, TV programming, and more. On the PlayStation Network, you can

✔ Shop online and download new games that are stored directly on your PS3's hard drive, check out demos of new games, and view high-definition trailers of new games and movies.

✔ Participate in free online head-to-head gaming competitions.

✔ Establish an online identity, build an avatar, participate in message boards, and do live text and voice chats.

✔ Surf the Internet. (Technically, surfing the Internet isn't part of the PlayStation Network — but don't let that stop you!)

You can find out more about the PlayStation Network at www.us.playstation.com.

Although the PlayStation Network is free, some games may require an additional subscription fee to play online.

PSP and Nintendo DS: Wi-Fi gaming to go

The Sony PSP (PlayStation Portable) is a portable, handheld gaming device. But wait — there's much more: The PSP is also an all-purpose media player that lets you store and view photos, play music, and even watch videos! Sony currently offers two PSP systems: The PSPgo, the latest (and cheapest) model, which skips the UMD optical drive found in the original PSP, and the PSP-3000 (often marketed as just "PSP"), which is the most recently updated version of the original. Both versions of the PSP include a built-in Wi-Fi (802.11b) adapter that lets you connect to wireless networks so you can play online games against others on your network or over the Internet, or browse your favorite Web sites using the built-in Web browser! With the PSP-3000, you can even use your handheld to make Skype phone calls over the Internet.

The Nintendo DS platform is Nintendo's answer to the Sony PSP. Like the PSP, the DS is a portable handheld gaming device with multimedia and Wi-Fi capabilities. But unlike the PSP, the DS has *two screens* (the lower screen is touch sensitive for game control)! The DS family currently consists of four models: the mainstay DSi (an improved successor to the original DS); the larger DSi XL; the budget-priced DS Lite (which is slightly smaller than the DSi and won't play newer games that have been designed for the DSi); and the recently released Nintendo 3DS (which, as the name implies, renders 3D graphics without the need for special glasses).

All four DS devices, as mentioned here, include built-in Wi-Fi networking and utilize Nintendo's Wi-Fi Connection service. With this service (and a game that supports it), you can connect directly to other DS users nearby (via your Wi-Fi adapter and without using a wireless router) and play multiplayer games head-to-head. Depending upon the game, you can even do this with only one game cartridge — for example, the popular *Mario Kart* game lets multiple players race each other with the cartridge in only one DSi. Pretty cool stuff!

Movies on your TV, courtesy of your gaming console

All three of the major gaming consoles now support the delivery of Internet-based movie and TV content to your TV screen. The biggest news here is that each of these consoles supports a downloadable Netflix application. (See more details at www.netflix.com.) With just your Internet connection and a monthly service plan that starts at only $7.99 per month, you can watch any of tens of thousands of movies and thousands of TV shows on demand — any time you want, as much as you want.

Not all movies are available on this streaming plan, so if you want to watch the latest releases, you'll need to upgrade your monthly plan to include DVDs or Blu-ray discs. Netflix isn't your only choice; you can also use your console to access YouTube videos or other movie services like Vudu (www.vudu.com; available on the PlayStation 3) or Hulu Plus (www.hulu.com; supported on the Xbox 360 and PlayStation 3).

You can also access Netflix, Vudu, Hulu Plus, and other video services from a networked Blu-ray disc player or television, if you have one (as well as on your computer, tablet, or smartphone). Almost all new Blu-ray disc players support these services over a wired or wireless connection, and an increasing number of TVs also include this functionality. Most TVs and Blu-ray disc players support only wired connections, so you'll need either a wireless Ethernet adapter or an Ethernet cable in your home theater to make this work.

Wii

Nintendo's online services include numerous channels, including the Wii Channel, Nintendo Channel, Mii Channel, Internet Channel, Photo Channel, Wii Shop Channel, and others.

Similar to the online offerings from Sony and Microsoft, Nintendo provides lots of great online content and capabilities for the Wii. You can preview and download new games, shop online, browse the Internet, and much more.

Xbox Live

Xbox Live (www.xboxlive.com) lets you use your Xbox 360 to get connected with friends online, download and play games, and quickly access games, music, movies, and more!

Xbox Live is no longer available for the original Microsoft Xbox.

The basic service, *Xbox Live Free* (formerly known as *Xbox Live Silver*) lets you voice chat, preview games, watch television and movies (rental fees apply) in high definition, download games and add-ons, and build a Gamertag and Avatar.

Xbox Live Gold adds party and video chat, multiplayer gaming, streaming movies and television (requires Netflix and Sky Player subscriptions, respectively), and Facebook, Twitter, ESPN, and more. An Xbox Live Gold account costs about $10 monthly or $60 annually.

Finally, Microsoft has added the *Xbox Live Gold Family Pack* which allows you to manage your family memberships and settings, view family usage reports, and earn Microsoft Point Allowances and discounts for your family. An Xbox Live Gold Family Pack membership costs $100 annually and gives you up to four Xbox Live Gold accounts.

PC Gaming

You may be surprised to read that although gaming consoles are all the hype, PC gaming is still considered to be on the cutting edge among gaming enthusiasts. Although you can get started with PC gaming on practically any modern PC (or Mac), if you're a hardcore gamer (or an aspiring hardcore gamer) you're going to need a bigger boat — uhh, PC! Some important hardware components to consider in a gaming PC with all the bells and whistles are the video card, processor and memory, sound, and game controllers.

Before you start shopping, it's important to figure out what types of games you're going to play on your PC. If you're a "casual" gamer who wants to play solitaire or Angry Birds, well any PC will do. If you're interested in the latest "first person shooter" games like Call of Duty: Black Ops, with intense and intricate graphics, you're going to need the latest and greatest CPU, graphics adapter and plenty of memory for the best results.

If you've got a specific game in mind, look on the box (or better yet, the game developer's Web site) for minimum requirements. Every manufacturer will list a set of minimum requirements and most will also provide an optimum configuration for best performance. If your PC doesn't quite meet the requirements you may find that the game won't work at all, or simply that it plays only at a lower resolution or frame rate.

Video card

PC games use the most powerful high-resolution graphics technology available, which is why they are so appealing to gaming enthusiasts. But to experience those incredible graphics, you'll need an equally powerful high-resolution video card. The video card in your PC affects the overall quality of your gaming experience: what games you can play, how they look, and how well they run.

A powerful video card lets you take advantage of higher screen resolutions (more colors and pixels), special graphic effects and enhancements, and faster frame rates (how smooth or choppy your games run). Typically, there is a tradeoff between quality and speed: Higher resolution and more graphic effects usually result in slower frame rates. You can adjust these settings to suit your preferences.

Generally speaking there are two types of video graphics cards:

- **Integrated graphics:** These are video cards that are built into the motherboard of a computer (most often in a notebook computers, but also in less expensive desktop computers) and use a portion of the computer's main RAM (random access memory) for video processing. These cards are typically less powerful and less suited for hardcore gaming. If your computer has integrated graphics, there's likely no way to upgrade it.

- **Discrete graphics:** These are separate cards, connected to the PC's motherboard via the PCI Express or other bus, with their own video RAM or memory. (You'll know you have this if your PC's specs say something like NVIDIA GeForce or ATI Radeon.)

In most desktop computers (those with discrete graphics), it's possible to upgrade your video card when your gaming requirements require you to do so or when newer, bigger, and better cards become available. In laptop computers, even those with discrete graphics cards, this typically isn't possible.

There are literally hundreds of video cards available on the market, with manufacturers continuously bringing out new models and new variants of existing models. So it's impossible to just say "buy this one or that one" in a book. But generally look for features such as:

- **Lots of memory:** For casual gaming, at least 256MB (512 Megabytes is better); for hardcore gaming, look for at least a gigabyte of memory.

- **DirectX support:** DirectX is Microsoft's graphics technology for Windows. DirectX 11 is the latest version, and you should look for a card that supports this version if your games require it.

- **Clock speeds:** Just as PC CPUs are rated at their *clock speed* (a measurement of calculations per second, in GHz, like a 2.2 GHz Intel Core 2 Duo), so are video cards. You can find measurements of the memory bus, the core bus speed of the card, and the *shader* (the CPU within the graphics card). In these cases, a bigger number means a faster card, compared to a similar card with lower numbers.

In the end, even if you know all of the stats, its hard to really compare video cards just by the numbers. Your best bet is to look on the Web, on sites like Tom's Hardware (www.tomshardware.com) and look for actual tests of the cards on games you're interested in playing.

As mentioned earlier, when you're shopping for a video card, be sure to check the minimum and recommended requirements for any games you currently own or plan to play.

Processor and memory

A fast processor and lots of memory is important for more than just gaming. The processor and memory affects the overall speed and performance of your PC. Most newer PCs now have multiple-core processors and at least 2 gigabytes (GB) of memory. (4GB is increasingly becoming the minimum and 8 or more GB of memory is probably a good range.)

Processors are usually not the bottleneck in PC game performance. You'll typically get a bigger performance lift by investing in a better video card (see the preceding section) or more memory rather than a faster processor. That having been said, if you're looking to do some serious gaming, you should consider a PC with one of Intel or AMD's latest CPUs. In the case of Intel, this means a processor from the Core family (Core i3, i5, and i7 — the higher the number the more powerful the processor); for AMD, this means a processor from the Phenom and Phenom II product lines. For more casual gaming, Intel's older Core 2 Duo or AMD's Athlon processors are more than suitable.

Sound

Of course, having awesome graphics is only part of the complete PC gaming experience. You can't play realistic explosions and DVD-quality soundtracks through a PC speaker! You'll need to invest in a good multimedia sound card and some surround-sound speakers to get the most out of your gaming PC.

For most folks, the sound cards built into any PC is good enough for gaming purposes, but if you're interested in hooking your gaming PC into a surround-sound system, you might wish to choose a PC (or upgrade an existing one) with a gaming-specific card that plugs into the PC's PCI Express bus. You can find such cards from manufacturers such as Creative Labs (www.soundblaster.com) or ASUS (usa.asus.com) for $50 to $100.

Game controllers

Most PC games can be played with a mouse and keyboard, but who wants to drive a Ferrari or fly a stealth fighter using the up-, down-, left- and right-arrow keys? There are lots of cool joysticks, steering wheels, and other gadgets that you can connect to your PC to provide a more complete gaming experience. Most gaming controllers connect to your PC via a USB cable, but you can also find Bluetooth wireless controllers.

Most PC games are configured to work with both a standard keyboard and mouse combination and with some sort of controller — exactly how this works is dependent upon the game itself. Luckily, most controllers work with Microsoft's Windows Human Interface Device specifications, which the games themselves also utilize. In most cases, you simply need to connect your controller to your PC, install any drivers that came with it, and then configure the settings within your game to let it know you're using a controller.

Check out CNET's GameSpot (www.gamespot.com) and IGN Entertainment's GameSpy (www.gamespy.com) for expert opinions and advice about the best PC gaming hardware.

Beyond the hardware mentioned here, connecting your gaming PC to your home network is really no different than connecting any other PC on your network. You can set up a wired or wireless connection and start playing!

To play your PC (and console) games online, you may need to configure your router and firewall in order to optimize your connections for the best possible game playing experience. There are also many home wireless routers and firewalls available that are specially designed for online gaming, mainly through their support of UPnP (Universal Plug and Play), which automatically configures the router and its firewall to allow connections to online gaming services.

Automating Your Entire Home

Advances in home automation technology, including lower hardware costs and new networking protocols, are making the home of the future possible today. By home automation, I'm talking about two related tasks: first, the *control* of devices in the home such as light switches, heating and AC controls, and appliances, and second, the automation of the operation of those devices — according to a schedule or in response to the situation. For example, you could program a system to turn lights on at a certain time of day, or to do so when a motion sensor detects someone entering a room or even when you've finished watching a movie and turned the TV off. Examples of home automation technologies and their possible uses include:

- **Refrigerators:** Using RFID (radio frequency identification) technology to identify the contents of your refrigerator, you can use your smartphone to build your shopping list while you're at the grocery store, surf the Internet for recipe ideas based on what you have in the fridge, manage your perishables and leftovers to better reduce spoilage, leave a note for your family on the refrigerator door's LCD screen, or stream a saved episode of *Emeril Live* to your refrigerator door so you can listen while you cook. Bam!

- **Ovens, bread makers, and coffee makers:** Automatically program and synchronize all of your clocks and schedules, download new recipes from the Internet, and get text or e-mail notifications when your Thanksgiving turkey, Christmas bread, or a fresh pot of coffee is ready!

- **Washing machines and dryers:** Download new wash-cycle programs from the Internet, check the status of your laundry online, and automatically notify the manufacturer or a repairman when a malfunction occurs.

- **Heating and cooling thermostat:** Remotely program your thermostat while you're away — in case you forgot to do it before leaving on an extended business trip or vacation.

- **Lighting and blinds:** Turn the lights on or off so you never have to come home to a dark house, and open or close your blinds to scare off potential burglars or help you reduce your energy bills.

- **Security cameras:** Monitor your front door or a nursery with wireless security cameras.

When shopping for network-capable home appliances, look for standard networking technologies and protocols, such as 802.11 wireless, Bluetooth, UPnP (Universal Plug and Play), and Ethernet or Powerline adapters.

For most folks, the first step into smart home (home automation) technologies is to create a wireless *control* network that (as its name implies) controls simple devices such as lights or blinds. There are two main wireless protocols for this type of home control, both of which are relatively widely supported by vendors:

✔ **ZigBee:** www.zigbee.org

✔ **Z-Wave:** www.z-wave.com

Both of these technologies are wireless, but they're different from (and don't interfere with) more familiar wireless technologies in the home like 802.11b/g/n Wi-Fi or Bluetooth. Both ZigBee and Z-Wave are low-power, relatively short-range wireless systems that use something called *mesh networking* to extend their reach throughout the home. Mesh networking is essentially the lily pad approach to networking, where a signal hops across multiple ZigBee or Z-Wave devices to get from point A to point B, just as a frog would jump across multiple lily pads to cross the pond. This means that the more devices you have in your home, the better coverage you'll have throughout the house, as there are more nodes in your mesh network to help transmit control signals.

There are a lot of vendors of ZigBee or Z-Wave systems on the market, ranging from fancy whole-home automation vendors like Control4 (www.control4.com) to companies that make electrical equipment like Leviton (www.leviton.com) to home theater vendors like Monster Cable (www.monstercable.com), which makes a popular universal programmable remote (the Home Theater and Lighting Controller) that incorporates Z-Wave for lighting control.

A great way to get started with wireless home control is with a kit like Schlage's (yep, the door lock company!) LiNK (http://link.schlage.com) starter kits. These kits start with remotely controllable door latch/lock devices (obviously, given who makes them!), but the kits can be easily expanded to include controllers for lights, drapes, thermostats, and other devices. Be careful, though, because once you start automating your home, you might not ever want to stop.

Keeping Your Home Safe

There are many home security solutions available today through professional security companies such as ADT, Broadview Security (formerly Brinks), GE Security, and others. Alternatively, you may elect to go the do-it-yourself route with an inexpensive wired or wireless kit that includes motion sensors, alarms, control panels, key fobs, and even wireless cameras. Many of these systems can be connected to your home network to provide remote monitoring capabilities for you when you're away from home.

An always-on DSL connection may potentially interfere with your alarm panel's internal modem, which uses analog phone lines. This interference may prevent the alarm panel from reliably communicating with the emergency response center. Your alarm company can install a DSL line filter to prevent any interference. Although a DSL line filter is simple to install, you should let your alarm company provide and install the line filter to ensure it is installed correctly and that your alarm system continues to work properly.

Traditionally, alarm systems had to be connected to an analog phone line (or, as the folks in the telephone business call them, *POTS* — Plain Old Telephone Service). Lots of folks these days have switched to broadband Voice-over-Internet-Protocol (VoIP) phone services like Vonage or phone service from their cable company, and many more have switched to mobile-only voice services. In these cases, you're not going to have a POTS line for alarm monitoring. Luckily, many alarm monitoring services (for example, NextAlarm; www.nextalarm.com) are now offering monitoring services over broadband connections or even over cellular network connections. So don't feel like you need to keep that expensive extra landline that's only used for your alarm — you can switch to broadband and cut the cord.

Configuring Your Gaming Console for Wireless Networking

In the tasks that follow, I show you the actual settings you'll need to configure to connect your gaming console to your home network and to the Internet. There's nothing magical or complicated here — the things you need to know (like your SSID and WPA passphrase) to configure a PC, Mac, iPhone, or any other device on your wireless network are the things you need to know and enter when you configure your gaming console. The only real difference is that you're doing it on the TV screen. So you won't need your reading glasses!

Configuring the Wii

Stuff You Need to Know

Toolbox:

✔ Nintendo Wii and Wii remote, already connected to your TV or home theater

✔ Your wireless network SSID and WPA passphrase

 **Time Needed:**

5 minutes

To set up wireless networking on your Wii, make sure you know your network's SSID and WPA passphrase before you begin. I'm going to assume that your Wii is already connected to your TV and/or home theater gear and turned on — if it's not, do that first! To get started, just do the following.

Warning: The wireless system in the Wii supports only the 802.11b and g standards. If your home network uses the 802.11n standard (the current standard), you will need to make sure that it is operating on the 2.4 GHz band (in the case of *dual-band* home routers), or your Wii will not be able to "talk" to it. For the majority of folks, your network will be operating on the 2.4 GHz band, but if you had a choice when you configured your network and you chose 5 GHz instead of 2.4 GHz, you'll need to change that setting. If you have a *simultaneous dual-band* router, you won't have to worry.

1. Using your Wii Remote, press the A button to click the Wii button in the bottom-left corner of the screen, and then click Wii Settings.

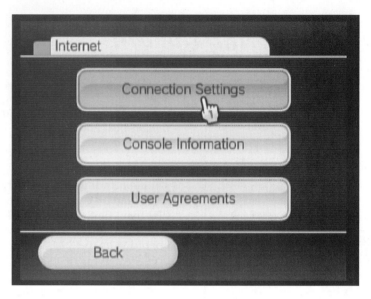

2. On the Wii Settings screen, navigate to the second page of settings (Settings 2) and select Internet by pointing to it it with your Wii Remote and clicking the A button. The Internet screen opens.

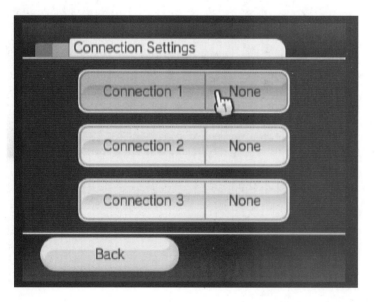

3. Select Connection 1, and then select Wireless Connection when it appears onscreen.

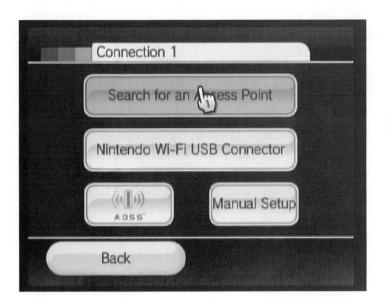

4. On the next screen, select Search for an Access Point. Your Wii will find all nearby Wi-Fi networks broadcasting their SSID and display them on your screen.

5. Select your network by clicking it. If you've enabled encryption on your network, you'll be prompted to enter your WEP or WPA passphrase. Do so using the onscreen keyboard and your Wii remote, and then select OK.

```
Connection 1

Triton

WPA2-PSK (AES)    This access point is secure.

Input the password or key.
**********

Change Security Settings

Back                          OK
```

6. Click OK, and your Wii saves your settings and connects to your network and to Nintendo's servers to test your connection.

   If your Wii reports any issues with the test, you're given some cryptic Wii Support Code. The most common issue is a mistyped passphrase, which will return a support code of 51330 or 52130 — check that you've typed the passphrase correctly. If you get a different support code, go to www. nintendo.com and search with the phrase *Wii connection error codes* to find a long list that will let you troubleshoot whatever indecipherable code Nintendo provides you.

7. That's all you need to do. Your Wii will automatically connect to your network each time you turn it on.

Configuring the PlayStation 3

Stuff You Need to Know

Toolbox:

✔ PlayStation 3 and controller, already connected to your TV or home theater

✔ Your wireless network SSID and WPA passphrase

Time Needed:

5 minutes

Like the Wii discussed in the previous task, the PlayStation 3 (PS3) comes configured out of the box, ready for use on a wireless network. So assuming that your PS3 is already connected to your TV/home theater and turned on, you can get up and running on your wireless network in just a couple of minutes. To do so, follow these steps.

Warning: The wireless system in the PlayStation 3 supports only the 802.11b and g standards. If your home network uses the 802.11n standard (the current standard), you will need to make sure that it is operating on the 2.4 GHz band (in the case of *dual-band* home routers) or your Wii will not be able to "talk" to it. For the majority of folks, you'll be using the 2.4 GHz band for your network, but if you had a choice when you configured your network and you chose 5 GHz instead of 2.4 GHz, you'll need to change that setting. If you have a *simultaneous dual-band* router, you won't have to worry.

1. Using your controller, navigate to the Settings menu on your PS3, and then open the Network Settings menu.

TIP If you're new to using the PlayStation 3, you might not know which of the buttons on the controller to use to move around your screen and select things. On the right side of the controller, the X button is used to select something on the screen and perform that action or open that menu, while the O button is used to cancel an operation. The directional keys (there are four of them) on the left side of the controller are used to move around the screen to select things (like using a mouse to move your cursor on a PC screen).

2. When the Network Settings menu opens, select Internet Connection Settings. If your system asks you if you want to be disconnected from the Internet (perhaps you'd previously had a wired connection on your PS3), select the Yes option.

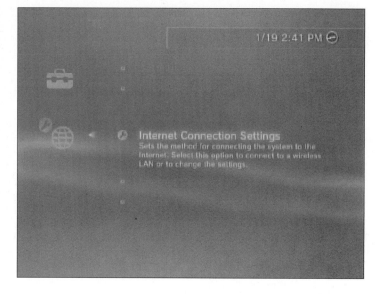

3. Select the Easy option when prompted, and then select the Wireless option.

4. Click the Scan option and look for your wireless network's SSID to appear on the screen. Don't be surprised if you see a bunch of networks — especially if you live in an apartment, condo, or just a neighborhood where the houses are relatively close together.

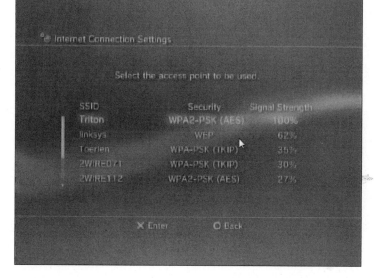

5. When you find your network's SSID listed on your TV screen, select it by clicking it with your controller.

6. Next, select the security you use on your network. You can choose None, WEP, or WPA-PSK/WPA2-PSK, so choose the one appropriate for your network. Again, I highly recommend that you use WPA on your network if possible.

7. If you've chosen an option other than None in the previous step, you'll be prompted to enter your WEP or WPA passphrase. Do so now, using your controller and the onscreen pop-up keyboard. Note that for (somewhat silly — I mean who's gonna be looking over your shoulder in your own family room?) security purposes, the characters you enter will turn to asterisks (*) after you enter them, so it can be hard to keep track. When you're done, click the Save button.

8. Now you're ready to test your
wireless Internet connection. Do so
by selecting the Test Connection
option on your screen. Your PS3
will connect to your wireless
network and then to a test server
on the Internet and confirm that
everything's working okay. If you
get any error messages, your PS3
will prompt you for changes you
need to make — most of the time,
it's something simple like a
mistyped passphrase.

9. That's it; you're done. Your PS3 will automatically connect to your
network whenever you turn it on.

Configuring the Xbox 360

Stuff You Need to Know

Toolbox:

✔ Xbox 360 and controller, already connected to your TV or home theater

✔ Microsoft Xbox 360 Wireless N Adapter (unless you have the Xbox 360 S console)

✔ Your wireless network SSID and WPA passphrase

Time Needed:
5 minutes

Most Xbox 360 consoles require you to buy and install Microsoft's Xbox 360 Wireless N Adapter, which plugs into the back of your Xbox 360 console. If you need to use this adapter, you can find complete installation instructions at the following URL: http://support. microsoft.com/kb/907330. If you have the new Xbox 360 S console, you can skip this step because your Xbox console has 802.11n networking already built in.

Remember: The Xbox 360 Wireless N Adapter, unlike the Wi-Fi built into the Wii or PlayStation 3, supports *dual-band* operation on both the 2.4 and 5 GHz bands. The Wi-Fi adapter built into the Xbox 360 S, however, supports operation on only the 2.4 GHz band — so you'll either need to ensure that your home network's router is operating on that band or buy the adapter if you want to (or must) use 5 GHz. When you install the Microsoft adapter in an Xbox 360 S, the internal wireless adapter will automatically turn itself off.

Once you have your wireless adapter situation resolved and your Xbox 360 console connected to your TV or home theater, you can connect your console to your network by performing the following steps. (They're really simple; trust me!)

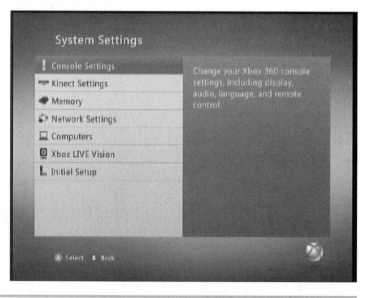

1. Using your Xbox controller, navigate to the My Xbox menu and select Console Settings. Use your controller to navigate down the menu and select Network Settings.

If you're setting up the Xbox 360 for your kids and don't know how to use the controller (I get it; it's got a *lot* of buttons), here's a short primer of the buttons you really need to worry about. On the left side, you'll see a four-way directional button (known as a *D-pad)* that lets you maneuver around the screen to select menu items. In the middle, you'll see a single, lit button with a stylized X on it: This is the Guide button, used to turn the console on and off and to open the Guide or system settings. On the right side, you'll see four buttons (A, B, X, and Y) used to take actions on the screen. Typically there will be a guide onscreen for which button to use for a particular action (for example, A to save, B to go back). If you're in doubt, the A button is usually your first choice to select a menu item that you've highlighted on the screen with D-Pad.

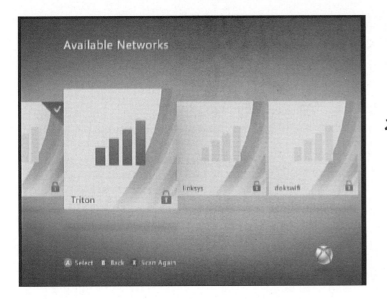

2. You'll be prompted to select your wireless network from the list of SSIDs that appears on the screen.

3. Select your network and, when prompted, enter your network security credentials (your WEP or WPA passphrase), and click Done.

TIP

If you weren't prompted to select a network in Step 3, click the Configure Network option and then the Basic Settings tab. In the screen that appears, select the Wireless Mode button and then click Scan for Networks. Find your network's SSID in the list that appears and select it.

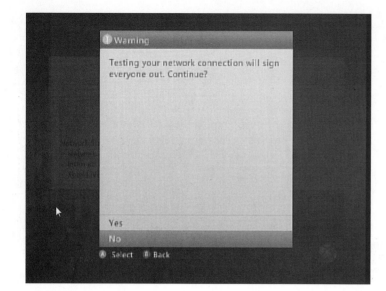

4. Your console will connect to your home network and the Internet and will then connect to an Xbox Live server to confirm the connection is working correctly. If you're so prompted, select Yes to log out of your account and begin the test.

5. If your connection fails in any way, your console will prompt you with troubleshooting steps. The most common issue you'll run into is a mistyped passphrase. (Hey, it's hard to type alphanumeric characters on the screen without a keyboard!)

Adding TVs and Blu-ray disc players to your network

As mentioned earlier in the chapter, many HDTVs and Blu-ray disc players now include wireless networking — either through built-in wireless adapters or with an optional plug-in USB network adapter. The process of configuring these devices to connect to your wireless network largely mirrors that discussed in the tasks for adding gaming consoles to your network. In other words, go into the settings menu of the device, select the networking settings, find the wireless option, use the menu options on your screen to search for and select your network, and — finally — enter your security credentials.

Unfortunately (for all of us) every manufacturer has its own unique spin on what happens in its own products' setup interface and process. So I can't give you specific step-by-step instructions here. Keep in mind the basic steps, pay attention when you enter your WPA passphrase, and you should be fine. I have faith in you!

Part IV
Keeping Your Network Safe and Healthy

The 5th Wave   By Rich Tennant

"We should cast a circle, invoke the elements, and direct the energy. If that doesn't work, we'll read the manual."

In this part . . .

At one time, it was nearly impossible to say "Windows" and "security" in the same sentence while keeping a straight face. No longer! With Windows 7, there are many great security features and enhancements that make it the most secure and stable Microsoft operating system yet.

In this part, you learn about Internet security threats and how Windows 7 features like the Action Center, Windows Firewall, Windows Defender, Windows Update, and Backup and Restore can help you keep your computer and network safe.

Chapter 11

Inside the Action Center

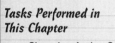
The Action Center is a nifty new feature in Windows 7 that monitors various security and maintenance-related items on your computer. It helps you keep your computer up to date and notifies you when there is an issue — without constantly nagging you, as in previous versions of Windows!

The Action Center Notification Icon

The Action Center appears as a small white flag in the notification area of your system tray (lower-right corner of your Windows desktop, next to the clock). See Figure 11-1.

Figure 11-1: The Action Center icon in the system tray.

If you move your mouse pointer over the Action Center flag without clicking it, a small tooltip pops up, either telling you there are no issues (see Figure 11-2) or indicating the number of relatively minor issues (see Figure 11-3).

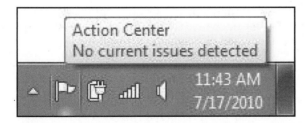

Figure 11-2: The Action Center tooltip — no issues.

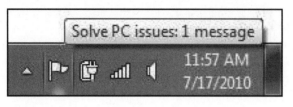

Figure 11-3: The Action Center tooltip — minor issues.

When there's a security or maintenance issue that requires attention, a small red *x* appears on the Action Center flag. See Figure 11-4.

Figure 11-4: The Action Center warning icon in the system tray.

When an important security or maintenance issue first occurs, in addition to the small red *x* appearing on the Action Center flag, a notification pops up telling you about the issue — and in some cases allowing you to fix the issue by simply clicking the notification. See Figure 11-5.

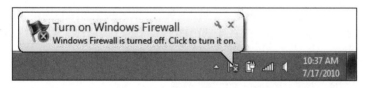

Figure 11-5: The Action Center notification for important issues.

By default, the Action Center monitors the following security and maintenance items:

✓ **Security messages**

- *Windows Update:* Microsoft regularly releases updates, fixes, patches, and drivers to the Windows operating system to constantly improve performance and stability, and to address newly discovered security risks. See Chapter 13 for more on Windows Update.

- *Internet security settings:* Internet Explorer security options are monitored by the Action Center. You can change these settings in Internet Explorer by going to the Tools menu and clicking Internet Options.

- *Network firewall:* Firewalls are integral to the security of your computer and network. I cover Windows Firewall in Chapter 12.

- *Spyware and related protection:* Spyware and adware are ubiquitous on the Internet today, thanks in large part to high-speed home Internet connections. Windows Defender helps protect your computer and network from these security threats, and I cover it in Chapter 12.

- *User Account Control:* This is where you change your notification settings, which I tell you how to do in this chapter.

- *Virus protection:* Antivirus software remains one of the most basic and important pieces of security software necessary to protect your computer and network.

✔ **Maintenance messages**

- *Windows Backup and Restore:* Helps you recover your computer and personal files when a virus inevitably wreaks havoc or a newly installed application decides not to play nice. Backup and Restore is covered in Chapter 14.

- *Windows Troubleshooting:* Windows 7 has many helpful tools for helping you troubleshoot problems. See Chapter 18 for a look at some of the most useful.

- *Check for updates:* Windows isn't the only software that is subject to security patches and bug fixes. This option allows Windows to automatically look for updates to common software such as Microsoft Office.

An Overview of the Action Center

When all is well in Windows, there isn't much to do in the Action Center. If you open the Action Center, you'll see the status of various items that it is monitoring, but there aren't many configuration changes you can make. See Figure 11-6. (I tell you how to open the Action Center in the task that follows.)

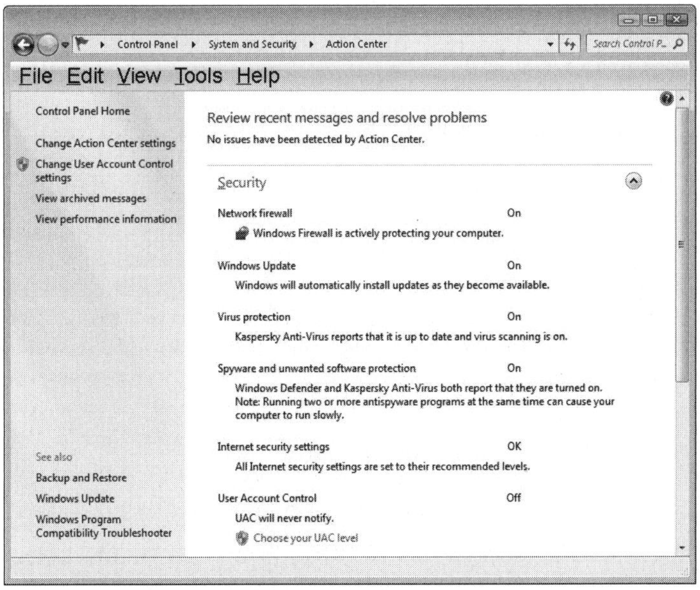

Figure 11-6: The Action Center with no issues detected.

However, when things are amiss, the Action Center makes it quick and easy for you to fix things. The Action Center identifies problems and indicates their relative importance with a red or yellow bar to the left. In many cases, correcting the issue is as simple as clicking the button to the right of the issue description (for example, turning on Windows Firewall). See Figure 11-7.

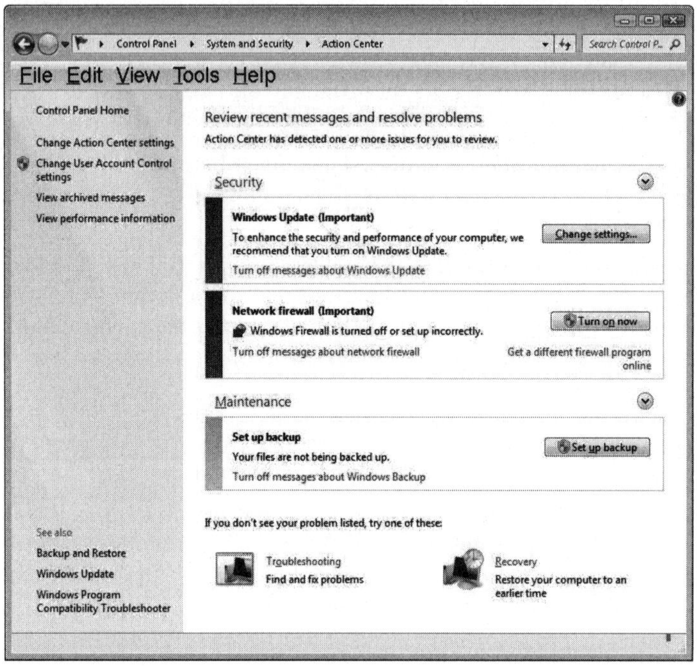

Figure 11-7: The Action Center with issues that need attention.

Changing Action Center Settings

Stuff You Need to Know

Toolbox:
- Computer running Windows 7

Time Needed:
5 minutes

Generally, you should enable monitoring of all of the default items in the Action Center. However, there may be situations in which you decide to turn off certain monitoring. For example, if you install a firewall, antispyware program, or backup software other than the ones included with Windows 7, you may want to turn off monitoring for those items if the Action Center doesn't recognize them. Otherwise, the Action Center will incorrectly indicate that these items are not enabled or are out of date.

1. From the Control Panel, click System and Security.

2. Click Action Center.

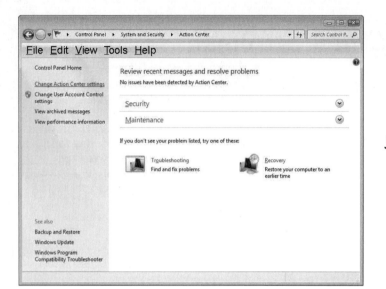

3. In the left pane, click Change Action Center Settings.

4. Select the items you would like Action Center to monitor for you and click OK.

Changing Customer Experience Improvement Program Settings

Stuff You Need to Know

Toolbox:

✔ Computer running Windows 7

Time Needed:

5 minutes

The Windows Customer Experience Improvement Program quietly collects information such as:

Computer hardware configuration: Including the number of processors your computer has and how your screen resolution is set

Performance and reliability: Including data regarding how quickly a program launches when you start it

System use: Including whether you use Microsoft programs such as Internet Explorer or Windows Media Player and how many folders do you typically create on the desktop

Periodically (about every 19 hours), an encrypted file containing all the information that has been collected is sent to Microsoft. There is no way for you to inspect the contents of the file or selectively limit what information is sent or when, and you are not notified when it is sent — it's all or nothing.

The goal of the program is to help Microsoft improve Windows. Although Microsoft does not use the information to identify or contact you, you may not be entirely comfortable with the idea of Microsoft covertly collecting this type of information. If this doesn't sound like something you care to voluntarily participate in, follow these steps:

1. From the Control Panel, click System and Security.

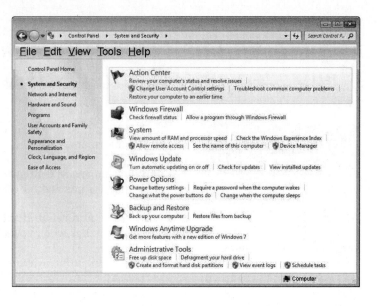

2. Click Action Center.

3. In the left pane, click Change Action Center Settings.

Turn messages on or off

For each selected item, Windows will check for problems and send you a message if problems are found.
How does Action Center check for problems?

Security messages

☑ Windows Update   ☑ Spyware and related protection

☑ Internet security settings ☑ User Account Control

☑ Network firewall   ☑ Virus protection

Maintenance messages

☑ Windows Backup   ☑ Check for updates

☑ Windows Troubleshooting

Related settings

Customer Experience Improvement Program settings

Problem reporting settings

Windows Update settings

OK   Cancel

4. Under Related Settings, click Customer Experience Improvement Program Settings.

5. Click No, I Don't Want to Participate in the Program and click Save Changes.

Customer Experience Improvement Program

Do you want to participate in the Windows Customer Experience Improvement Program?

The program helps Microsoft improve Windows. Without interrupting you, it collects information about your computer hardware and how you use Windows. The program also periodically downloads a file to collect information about problems you might have with Windows. The information collected is not used to identify or contact you.

Read the privacy statement online

○ Yes, I want to participate in the program.

● No, I don't want to participate in the program.

Save Changes   Cancel

Changing Problem Reporting Settings

Stuff You Need to Know

Toolbox:

✔ Computer running Windows 7

Time Needed:

5 minutes

Windows Problem Reporting (also known as Error Reporting) collects information from your computer when a hardware or software problem occurs and sends it to Microsoft. Unlike the Customer Experience Improvement Program, Windows Problem Reporting is a triggered event. It creates and sends a problem report only when you encounter a hardware or software problem. Information included in the problem report typically includes the name and version of the program that encountered the problem, when it occurred, and other factors that may have contributed (such as other programs that may also have been running). If a solution to the problem is available, Microsoft will notify you. Otherwise, you may be asked to provide additional information to help Microsoft create a solution to the problem. To configure your Problem Reporting settings, follow these steps:

1. From the Control Panel, click System and Security.

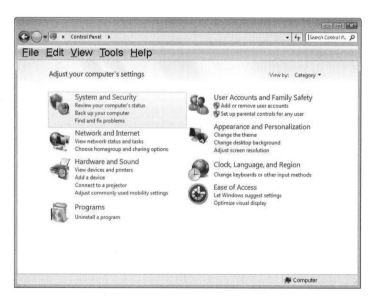

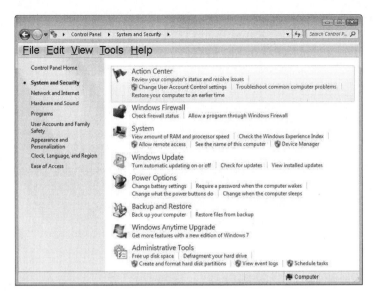

2. Click Action Center.

3. In the left pane, click Change Action Center Settings.

4. Under Related Settings click Problem Reporting Settings.

5. Select the setting you prefer. It's generally best to leave it set to Automatically Check For Solutions, which is the default setting. However, if you want more control over what your computer does when a problem occurs you might choose a different setting, such as Each Time a Problem Occurs, Ask Me Before Checking For Solutions.

6. From this screen, you can also exclude certain programs from the Windows Problem Reporting program. Click Select Programs to Exclude from Reporting.

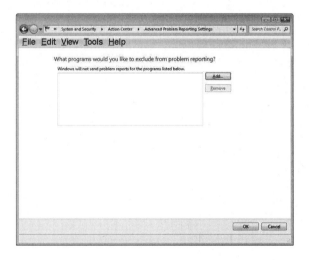

7. Click Add and select any programs that you want to exclude from reporting, and then click OK. For example, you may have a program that you know is prone to errors, and rather than having it check for a solution every time the error occurs, you may prefer to just ignore it and continue working.

8. Click OK to save your settings.

Changing User Account Control Settings

Stuff You Need to Know

Toolbox:
- Computer running Windows 7

Time Needed:
5 minutes

User Account Control (UAC) notifies you before computer changes that require an administrator account are made. There are four possible settings as follows:

Always notify. This is the most secure option. It notifies you anytime a program tries to make changes to your computer or to Windows settings. When you are notified of a pending change, your desktop is dimmed (to prevent other programs from running until a decision is made), and you must either approve or deny the change in the UAC dialog box.

Notify me only when programs try to make changes to my computer. Notifies you anytime a program tries to make changes to your computer or if a program outside of Windows attempts to make changes to a Windows setting.

Notify me only when programs try to make changes to my computer (do not dim my desktop). Same as the previous setting, except the desktop is not dimmed, which may allow some malicious programs to alter the appearance of the dialog box.

Never notify. This is the least secure setting. If you're logged on as a standard user, changes that require administrator permissions will be denied. If you're logged in as an administrator, those changes will be automatically permitted, potentially exposing your computer, network, and personal information to security risks.

Tip: Setting UAC to Never Notify requires you to reboot your computer in order for the setting to take effect.

Follow these steps to change the UAC notification setting:

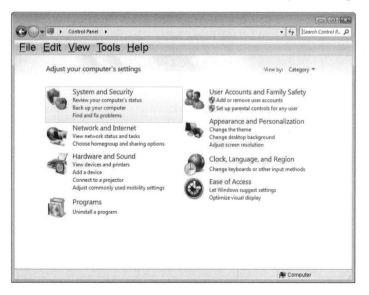

1. From the Control Panel, click System and Security.

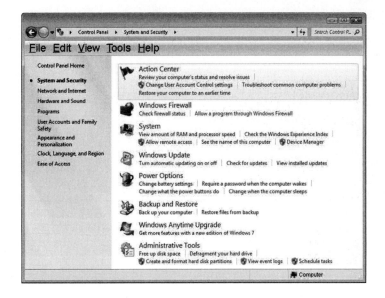

2. Click Action Center.

3. In the left pane, click Change User Account Control Settings.

4. Slide the vertical bar (on the left side) to your desired setting and click OK.

Viewing Archived Messages about Computer Problems

You've probably encountered error messages before that you didn't bother reading and just clicked OK or Ignore to continue working (perhaps more often than not!). However, if at some point you realize that maybe there really is a problem you need to take a closer look at, you can view archived error messages in Windows 7. To view archived messages for problems that are sent to Microsoft (configured in the Problem Reporting Settings). Follow these steps:

1. From the Control Panel, click System and Security.

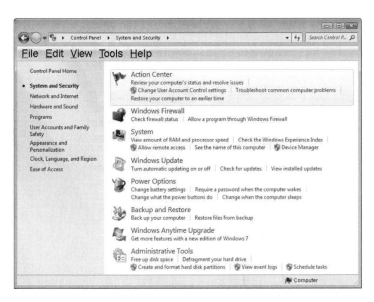

2. Click Action Center.

3. In the left pane, click View Archived Messages.

Accessing Other Control Panel Items

The Action Center also gives you quick, easy access to other Control Panel features, such as computer performance information. To view performance information, follow these steps:

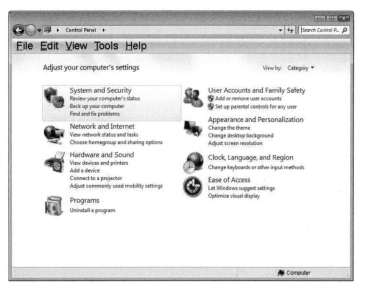

1. From the Control Panel, click System and Security.

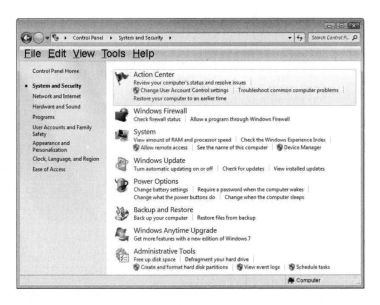

2. Under Action Center, you can access other Control Panel items, such as troubleshooting computer problems and restoring your computer to previous settings. Click Action Center to access still more Control Panel items.

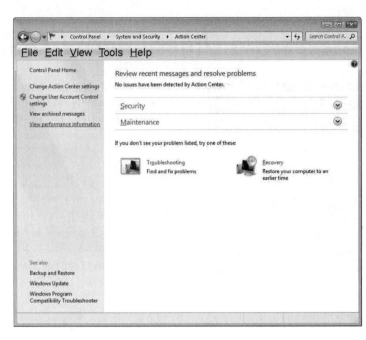

3. In the left pane, click View Performance Information.

4. From this screen, you can change numerous settings, including visual effects, indexing options, power settings, disk cleanup, and many others.

Hiding the Action Center Notification Icon

Stuff You Need to Know

Toolbox:
- ✔ Computer running Windows 7

Time Needed:
5 minutes

If the small white flag in your system tray absolutely annoys you, you have the option of hiding it, as follows:

1. Click the Up arrow to the left of the Action Center icon (white flag). Click Customize in the pop-up window that appears.

2. In the Notification Area Icons window, click the option bar to the right of Action Center. Choose Show Icon and Notifications, Hide Icon and Notifications, or Only Show Notifications, and then click OK.

3. To restore the default icon behaviors, click the link at the bottom of the Notification Area Icons window, and then click OK.

Chapter 12

Windows Firewall and Windows Defender

In the not-too-distant and relatively docile past, computer viruses were spread almost exclusively through floppy diskettes. In order for your computer to become infected with a virus, you had to insert an infected diskette into your PC's floppy disk drive and either run an infected program, open an infected file, or forget to take the diskette out before shutting down or rebooting your computer.

If, after all that, you managed to get your computer infected, the virus would at worst delete the contents of your hard drive or, more often than not, just cause your computer to start doing annoying (and perhaps mildly amusing) things like scroll a message or drive an animated ambulance across your monitor screen.

Today's viruses are much more sinister and are spread across the Internet with a speed and magnitude that makes earlier viruses seem more like a mild headache. Viruses, along with worms, Trojans, spyware, bots, and other assorted threats, are collectively known as *malware*.

Network security is perhaps the biggest challenge for anyone setting up a network, regardless of whether it's a small home network or a corporate network for a global enterprise. Internet threats are prolific, and new computer security risks are discovered and exploited literally every day.

Firewalls have long been a cornerstone of security in corporate networks that typically have a permanent ("always-on") connection to the Internet. As high-speed Internet access has become less expensive, always-on DSL or cable modem connections for home users have eclipsed old-fashioned dialup Internet connections in popularity — and thus the need for firewalls to protect home networks as well.

In addition to antivirus protection and firewalls, antispyware software is a necessary element in your security arsenal.

In this chapter, I explain malware and other Internet-borne threats such as spam, spoofing, and phishing attacks. Although these threats occur in cyberspace, they are perpetrated by very real criminals — including identity thieves and predators. I also explain how to protect your network with Windows Firewall and Windows Defender.

Defining Malware

Malware, short for *malicious software,* is software or code that is designed to damage files or entire computer systems, steal data, disrupt networks, or do generally bad things to computers, networks, and people. Malware consists of viruses, worms, Trojans, spyware, adware, backdoors, rootkits, and bots.

Viruses

Viruses are perhaps the most common and most well-known type of malware. A *virus* spreads by inserting a copy of itself into an executable program or file. The distinguishing characteristic of viruses versus other types of malware is that a virus requires a computer user to run the program or open the file that contains the virus in order for it to actively infect the computer. Traditionally, viruses have been spread via shared diskettes and files, but today they are increasingly spread via networks and e-mail attachments.

Worms

A *worm* is similar to a virus, but with these two important distinctions:

- It does not require a host program or file.
- It can replicate and infect computers without human action.

Worms typically take advantage of a known vulnerability or bug in a computer program or operating system.

Trojans

A *Trojan* or *Trojan horse* is malware that masquerades as legitimate software. Like a virus, a Trojan requires a computer user to actually install or run it. Once the Trojan has been installed or run, it can do extensive damage to a computer, delete files, steal data, and run other malware (such as viruses). Although it can spread a virus or worm, a Trojan does not replicate itself (or spread) to other systems. Trojans may also install a *backdoor* or a *rootkit* on an infected system, which provides a way for an attacker to covertly gain access to your system in order to steal data or do other damage in the future (even after you believe you have successfully removed the Trojan).

Spyware

Spyware quietly collects information about users and can be very difficult to detect. Spyware can be used to covertly monitor a computer user's activities or log keystrokes. Other spyware is less covert and may do very annoying things to a computer, such as

The worst virus ever!

You've no doubt received e-mails warning you about a virus that, according to the e-mail, Microsoft says is "the worst virus ever" and confirmed on Snopes.com. The virus will do unspeakable damage to your computer, blah, blah, blah. E-mail hoaxes are the poor man's dirty virus — the terrorism equivalent of al Qaeda lighting a bag of doggie poop on your front door step!

E-mail virus warnings are hoaxes 99.999 percent of the time. Your first clue should be the claim that "Microsoft says it is the worst virus ever." Microsoft doesn't warn users about viruses. That's the job of companies like Symantec and McAfee. (Although Microsoft does now offer antivirus software, it is still not that company's forte.)

Your next clue is "confirmed on Snopes. com." While Snopes.com is a great Web site for verifying or debunking various urban legends, it is not an antivirus or security Web site. If you go to the trouble of looking up your e-mail hoax on Snopes. com, you will most likely find that Snopes. com confirms it is an e-mail hoax.

The best advice when you receive an e-mail chain predicting the end of the Internet as you know it is to delete it. If you're still not certain that it's a hoax, look it up on a reputable security Web site such as www. symantec.com or www.mcafee.com. But whatever you do, don't forward the e-mail to everyone you know!

- ✔ Install other software.
- ✔ Redirect Web browsers to other Web pages.
- ✔ Disable antivirus software.
- ✔ Change computer settings.
- ✔ Slow down Internet connections and network activity.

Adware is a type of spyware that displays unsolicited advertisements, targeted to a computer user based on the information that spyware installed on the computer discovers.

Bots

A *bot* is similar to a worm in that it can spread itself without human interaction. Bots are commonly spread through instant messaging and chat. Unlike many other types of malware, a bot rarely announces its presence on an infected computer, instead relying on stealth to do its damage. A bot can do a host of bad things, including

- ✔ Logging keystrokes
- ✔ Stealing passwords
- ✔ Capturing network traffic
- ✔ Gathering personal or financial data
- ✔ Launching denial-of-service (DoS) attacks

- ✔ Relaying spam
- ✔ Spreading viruses
- ✔ Installing backdoors

Bots often connect back to a remote server (or servers) and allow an attacker to take control of an infected computer. Such compromised computers are known as *zombies* and are often part of a *botnet*, a network of literally thousands of zombie computers used to send out spam and other malware, as well as to cause widespread denial of service attacks (known as distributed denial-of-service, or DDoS, attacks) against targeted networks. Botnets have become one of the most ubiquitous threats on the Internet today.

Blended threats

Unfortunately, hackers and cybercriminals aren't one-dimensional. A *blended threat* combines a number of malware programs into one big threat, making it difficult to classify most malware as a simple virus, worm, Trojan, or other threat. Beyond semantics, a blended threat also makes it very difficult to detect and protect computers and networks from malware.

Protecting Your Network from Malware

Protecting your computers and home network from malware begins before you even connect to the Internet. Literally. Before you connect a new computer to your home network, you need to ensure that it has antivirus software installed and running (see Chapter 11), and that your network firewall or the Windows Firewall is on (see the "Turning Windows Firewall On or Off and Changing Notification Settings" task later in this chapter). The SoBig worm of 2003 infected vulnerable computers within a matter of *seconds,* when they connected to the Internet over dialup connections. With today's high-speed, always-on cable and DSL Internet connections, an unprotected computer connected to the Internet for any amount of time is a sitting duck.

Antivirus software

Antivirus software (now being commonly marketed as antimalware, endpoint protection, and Internet security software) is relatively inexpensive and protects computers and networks from many of the malware threats described in the preceding section. Most antivirus software uses definition files to detect new threats. In order to be effective, antivirus signatures must be frequently updated. (New viruses are discovered *every* day.) Best practices for configuring your antivirus software include the following:

- ✔ Enabling real-time scanning of files so they are scanned for viruses when downloaded or opened
- ✔ Enabling real-time protection to constantly monitor commonly infected areas of the computer's operating system

✔ Scheduling daily automatic updates of definition files

✔ Scheduling full-system scans on a daily basis (usually late at night when the computer is not in use, since full-system scans significantly slow your computer)

✔ Automatically cleaning or quarantining infected files and alerting you when a virus is detected

Popular antivirus software includes the following:

✔ **Symantec Norton AntiVirus:** Approximately $40 with one year subscription (www.symantec.com)

✔ **McAfee AntiVirus Plus:** Approximately $40 with one year subscription (www.mcafee.com)

✔ **Trend Micro Titanium Antivirus +:** Approximately $40 with one year subscription (www.trendmicro.com)

✔ **AVG Anti-Virus Free Edition:** Free (http://free.avg.com)

✔ **Malwarebytes' Anti-Malware:** Free (www.malwarebytes.org)

✔ **Microsoft Security Essentials:** Also free (www.microsoft.com/security_essentials)

A major problem with the effectiveness of antivirus software is the reactive nature of definition files. A definition cannot be written for a virus that doesn't yet exist. Therefore, a small window of vulnerability exists between the time a virus is first created — or in the wild, so to speak — and the time it takes for your antivirus software maker to create a new definition file for the virus and get it installed on your computers.

Antispyware software

Antispyware (and antiadware) software detects spyware/adware and cleans it from your computer. It also prevents it from getting infected in the first place when possible. Antispyware software works very similarly to antivirus software by using definition files to identify known spyware. Therefore, many of the same best practices and limitations of antivirus software (discussed earlier) are applicable to antispyware software as well. Many antivirus vendors bundle antispyware software into their antivirus products or offer it as an add-on module. Other effective (and reputable) antispyware programs include

✔ **Spybot – Search & Destroy:** Free (www.safer-networking.org)

✔ **Lavasoft Ad-Aware Free:** Free (www.lavasoft.com)

✔ **Microsoft Windows Defender:** Free and included with Windows 7

Many Trojans and spyware programs masquerade as antispyware software and actually disable genuine antivirus and antispyware programs. Be careful when downloading "antispyware" software!

Firewalls

Firewalls prevent attackers from gaining unauthorized access to your network and can protect your computers and network from some types of malware. You find out how to configure Windows Firewall to protect your network later in this chapter.

Security updates and fixes

Many malware programs take advantage of known security vulnerabilities that exist in operating systems and software. You may be thinking, "If they're known, why aren't they fixed?" Well, computer operating systems and software contain millions of lines of code, so it is inevitable that security vulnerabilities and bugs will exist. If every operating system or software application had to be perfect before it was sold or released to the public, we wouldn't have much software available to us today. Generally, as soon as a vulnerability or bug is discovered, the software developers get to work on a fix. (Although there is sometimes a brief period of denial that leads to risky delays — seriously.) Unfortunately, the fixes sometimes introduce new vulnerabilities or break earlier fixes, so patching and updating software is an ongoing (and vicious) cycle. In general, you should install any relevant software updates or fixes as soon as they are available. See Chapter 13 to learn more about keeping your computers up to date with the latest fixes and security patches.

E-mail Threats

Malware is frequently spread via e-mail, often appearing to come from someone you know and trust. As if that weren't enough, e-mail has some original threats of its own, including spam, spoofing, and phishing attacks.

Spam

Spam is the scourge of e-mail around the world. At times, it makes up as much as 95 percent of all e-mail on the Internet! Spammers get e-mail addresses from newsgroups, unscrupulous Web site operators who sell e-mail addresses to them, and malware that harvests e-mail addresses from hacked e-mail accounts. Spammers also guess e-mail addresses and sometimes just get lucky. Spam causes a number of issues, including these:

- **Network congestion:** Spam clogs your pipes — that is, your network pipes! Although e-mail is relatively small in size, receiving enough of it will cause congestion on your network. Worse yet, if your computer has become part of a botnet (see the earlier "Bots" section), you will definitely see a negative effect on your network as you could be *sending* thousands of spam e-mails to others!

- **Distraction and clutter:** Because spam can account for such a large volume of e-mail, legitimate e-mails may get buried in your inbox or inadvertently deleted along with all the spam.

- **Malware:** A large proportion of spam contains malware, or links to Web sites that contain malware.

As bad as most spam e-mail is, you might wonder why a spammer even bothers. A lot of has to do with spreading malware, but spamming is a multimillion dollar criminal enterprise. (Yes, it is illegal to send certain bulk unsolicited e-mails in the U.S. and many other countries.) Believe it or not, there are people who actually fall for this stuff and unwittingly send their hard-earned cash in response to an offer that is too good to be true. Think about it. Sending a spam e-mail to 10 million potential suckers costs a spammer absolutely nothing (especially since the majority of criminal spammers use zombie computers to serve up their spam). If only one-tenth of one percent of all of those potential suckers actually live up to their potential and send a spammer $100 for whatever miracle weight-loss pill or discount prescription drug or worse that they are hawking, the spammer makes one million dollars with no costs (unless the spammer gets caught)!

The best protection against spam (other than not using e-mail at all) is to use a spam filter. Of course, this may not be an option on your home network (although some Internet service providers offer spam filtering as an additional service). If you don't have a spam filter, you should also use any junk mail filtering options available in your e-mail software. Finally, never, ever, unsubscribe or reply to a spam e-mail. This only confirms to the spammer that your e-mail address is real, and it potentially opens a dialog with a professional con artist that will find a way to convince you to send him a little of your own hard-earned cash. You should only unsubscribe from spam that you know you've subscribed to before (such as a newsletter or department store e-mail list).

Spoofing

E-mail spoofing occurs when an attacker sends you an e-mail pretending to be someone you know. Spoofing is analogous to sending a letter to someone and forging the return address on the envelope. Unfortunately, e-mail spoofing is about that easy to do, and very difficult to trace to its real sender. You should always be leery of any e-mail you receive asking for money or sensitive information, even if it appears to be from someone you know and trust.

Phishing

Phishing (pronounced like *fishing*) e-mails have become a favorite weapon of identity thieves, and they are becoming increasingly difficult to spot. Most phishing e-mails purport to be from a banking or other financial institution (as well as Web sites such as PayPal), and every once in a while (and all too frequently) they get lucky and actually send an e-mail pretending to be from *your* bank. Phishing e-mails appear very authentic, and often include graphics and logos that are actually from your bank (for example, Bank of America or Chase). There may even be a link or two that actually takes you to your bank's Web site. But buried somewhere in that e-mail is a link that takes you to a malicious Web site. Even if you don't enter any personal information, simply clicking the link can infect your computer with data-stealing malware. Follow these best practices to reduce your risk of becoming a victim of identity theft:

✔ Never click a hyperlink in a suspect e-mail.

✔ Never reply to a suspect e-mail with personal information (such as social security numbers, account numbers, and passwords).

✔ Look for grammatical errors in the e-mail (but beware, identity thieves are getting more sophisticated).

✔ Contact your bank via telephone (get it from your bank's Web site, not from the e-mail you received) if you suspect fraud.

✔ If you subscribe to e-mail or text alerts from your bank or financial institution, you should be familiar with the format, content, and address of these messages. Be suspicious of anything you receive out of the norm.

✔ Watch for small charges on your financial statements — to avoid detection, a thief is more likely to steal a few dollars from thousands of bank accounts rather than several hundred dollars from a few bank accounts.

Social Engineering and Cyber Predators

Cyber predators, without a doubt, are among the worst cybercriminals. The stories of these vermin using social networks, chat, and other technology to victimize others are far too common. *Social engineering* is a low-tech method for gathering information about a potential victim. It includes techniques such as *shoulder surfing* (looking over someone's shoulder to observe her password), *dumpster diving* (digging through someone's garbage), and other tactics. In its more sinister form, it may include learning about your children's school and their friends or social activities. Always be wary of anyone that you or your family members communicate with over the Internet but do not already know personally — particularly over social networks such as Facebook and MySpace. Remember, cyberpredators and cybercriminals are real and will do real harm to real people if given the opportunity.

Understanding Windows Firewall

Almost all computers and networks (and for home networking purposes, *all* computers and networks) communicate by establishing connections between two hosts using an IP address and a port.

For example, your computer uses a Web browser to connect to a Web site, such as www.microsoft.com. Your computer must first resolve the IP address for Microsoft's Web server using the domain name system (DNS). Your computer sends a DNS request to the IP address of a DNS server — usually provided by your Internet service provider (ISP). DNS tells your computer that the IP address of www.microsoft.com is 207.46.232.182. Next, your computer attempts to connect to the IP address 207.46.232.182 on port 80 — the standard port used for the HyperText Transfer Protocol (HTTP), the language of the World Wide Web.

See Chapter 2 to find out more about IP addresses, ports, and the domain name system (DNS).

A firewall, at its most basic level, permits or denies communications between computers, between networks, or between computers and networks (for example, your home computer and the Internet) based on the firewall's configuration rules. Although there are many types of firewalls, the most common type of firewall (and the type used in Windows 7) permits or denies communications based on IP address and port information. Only connections that are explicitly allowed, using firewall rules, are permitted. Windows Firewall, by default, allows all *outbound* connections, and permits only *established inbound* connections (that is, an inbound connection that is in direct response to an outbound connection initiated from your computer or network).

There are firewalls protecting Microsoft's Web servers and your ISP's DNS servers. In the example here, in order for your computer to connect to Microsoft's Web servers, Microsoft must first create firewall rules to allow the communication. This is accomplished by creating a firewall rule that essentially says to allow any inbound IP address to connect to 207.46.232.182 (Microsoft's Web server) on port 80 (HTTP). Your ISP must create a similar rule on their firewall that essentially says to allow any inbound IP address to connect to its DNS servers on port 53 — which is the standard port for DNS.

Continuing with the above example, Windows Firewall permits your outbound DNS request to your ISP's DNS server, and your computer's outbound HTTP request to Microsoft's Web server. In your outbound request, your computer first sends the DNS request to your ISP's DNS server on port 53, and tells your ISP's DNS server on what port it will be listening for a response. Your computer selects a random port number between 49,152 and 65,535, and Windows Firewall automatically creates a temporary rule that allows an inbound connection from the IP address of your ISP's DNS server to the IP address of your computer, on that random port number. After the response is received (or if a response is not received within a specified period of time, say 30 seconds), the rule is automatically deleted from the firewall and the connection is again blocked. A similar process is then repeated to connect to Microsoft's Web server.

Understanding Windows Defender

Windows Defender is Microsoft's free antispyware program that is included in Windows 7. Like Windows Firewall, Windows Defender is enabled by default, and no configuration is required for it to begin protecting your computer. However, there are some settings you may want to customize, such as how often and when your computer is automatically scanned, what Windows Defender does when spyware is detected, and what you want scanned or excluded (such as certain programs, files, folders, or e-mail).

Viewing the Windows Firewall Dashboard

Stuff You Need to Know

Toolbox:

✔ Computer running Windows 7

Time Needed:

5 minutes

Windows Firewall is enabled by default, and is configured to allow all outbound connections and permit only inbound responses to established outbound connections. Thus, there is very little configuration that is required out of the box. To view the status of Windows Firewall, follow these steps.

1. From the Control Panel, click System and Security.

2. Click Windows Firewall.

3. The status of Windows Firewall is displayed for Home or Work (Private) Networks and Public Networks.

TIP

You can quickly check your firewall status from the Control Panel Systems and Security window (shown in Step 2) by clicking Check Firewall Status under Windows Firewall.

Allowing and Blocking Programs

Stuff You Need to Know

Toolbox:
- Computer running Windows 7
- Administrator account

Time Needed:
5 minutes

To allow or block specific programs, follow these steps:

1. From the Control Panel, click System and Security.

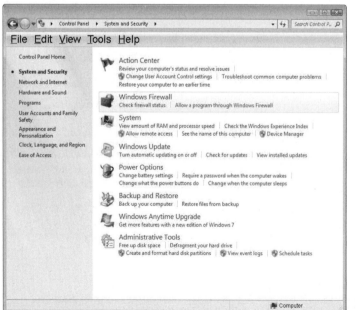

2. Click Windows Firewall.

3. In the left pane, click Allow a Program or Feature through Windows Firewall.

4. Under the list of allowed programs and features, select the program or feature you would like to modify by selecting or deselecting the check box to the left. Also select or deselect the check boxes to the right to allow the change to your Home/Work (Private) and Public network policy setting. Click OK.

5. If the program you need to allow through your firewall is not listed, click the Allow Another Program button and select it from the list of programs that appears or browse to the directory location of the program.

To learn more about a specific program or feature, select the program and click the Details button.

Turning Windows Firewall On or Off and Changing Notification Settings

Stuff You Need to Know

Toolbox:
- Computer running Windows 7
- Administrator account

Time Needed:
5 minutes

Like many Windows settings and features, Windows Firewall notifies you when certain events occur. For example, if a program is blocked, a pop-up window will alert you. For some people, this is fine. Others may find the notifications annoying and thus choose to disable the notification settings in Windows Firewall.

1. From the Control Panel, click System and Security.

2. Click Windows Firewall.

3. In the left pane, click Change Notification Settings or Turn Windows Firewall On or Off.

4. From that screen, you can turn the Windows Firewall on or off, block all incoming connections (overrides your allowed programs list), and turn off notifications when the Firewall blocks a program. Make your selections and click OK.

Restoring Your Windows Firewall Default Settings

There are a lot of options that can be configured in Windows Firewall, and it's possible to get lost in it all! Of course, when you lose track of what you've configured, the risk with Windows Firewall is that you may have inadvertently opened a big security hole in your network. To undo all of your changes and reset Windows Firewall to its default configuration, follow these steps:

1. From the Control Panel, click System and Security.

2. Click Windows Firewall.

3. In the left pane, click Restore Defaults.

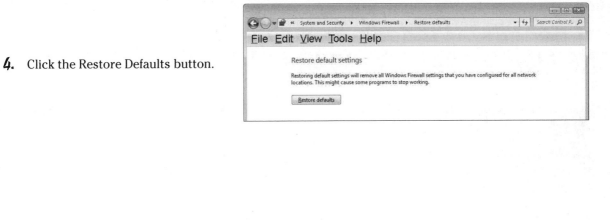

4. Click the Restore Defaults button.

5. Confirm that you want to restore your Windows Firewall to its default settings by clicking Yes.

Changing Windows Firewall with Advanced Security Properties

Stuff You Need to Know

Toolbox:
- Computer running Windows 7
- Administrator account

Time Needed:
10 minutes

There are many, many advanced properties that can be configured in Windows Firewall. You should not make changes here if you are a relative security neophyte. For those who have a specific advanced requirement, or are just plain adventurous, read on!

1. From the Control Panel, click System and Security.

2. Click Windows Firewall.

3. In the left pane, click Advanced Settings.

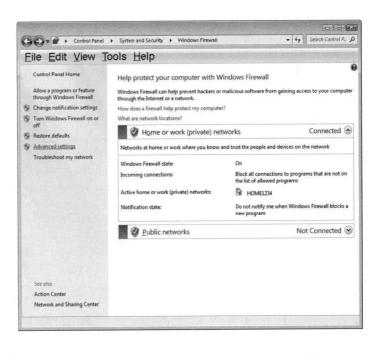

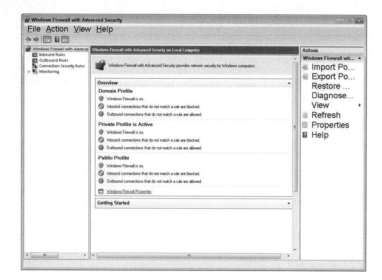

4. In the center pane under Overview, you can see how your firewall is currently configured. At the bottom of this window, click Windows Firewall Properties.

5. A window opens with separate tabs for each of the available profiles for your Windows Firewall (Domain, Private, and Public). The options for all three profiles are the same. Click the Private Profile tab. Ignore the IPsec Settings tab for now. IPsec settings are used in VPN profiles, which I cover in Chapter 9.

6. Under State, you can make the changes listed in the following table.

State Settings for Windows Firewall

Setting	Description
Firewall State	On (recommended) or Off.
Inbound Connections	Block (default, denies all inbound connections except those that are explicitly permitted), Block all connections (overrides any exceptions you may have created), or Allow (allows all inbound connections except those that are explicitly denied).
Outbound Connections	Allow (default, permits all outbound connections except those that are explicitly denied) or Block (denies all outbound connections except those that are explicitly permitted).
Protected Network Connections	Allows you to specify which network connections are protected by the firewall profile (for example, wireless network connection).

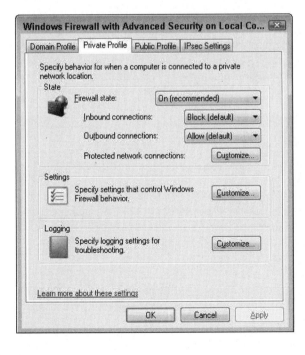

7. Under Settings, click Customize.

Customize Settings for the Private Profile

Specify settings that control Windows Firewall with Advanced Security behavior.

Firewall settings
Display notifications to the user when a program is blocked from receiving inbound connections.

Display a notification: `No`

Unicast response
Allow unicast response to multicast or broadcast network traffic.

Allow unicast response: `Yes (default)`

Rule merging
Merging of rules created by local administrators with rules distributed through Group Policy. This setting can only be applied through Group Policy.

Apply local firewall rules: `Yes (default)`

Apply local connection security rules: `Yes (default)`

Learn more about these settings

[OK] [Cancel]

8. In the Customize Settings for the Private Profile window, you can change whether firewall notifications are displayed, and whether unicast responses are allowed. You can also merge firewall rules (for example, rules that you create can be merged with rules applied to the entire network) if merging is enabled via a Group Policy. (Group Policies are beyond the scope of this book.) Make any changes desired and click OK.

9. Under Logging, click Customize.

Windows Firewall with Advanced Security on Local Co...

| Domain Profile | Private Profile | Public Profile | IPsec Settings |

Specify behavior for when a computer is connected to a private network location.

State

Firewall state: `On (recommended)`

Inbound connections: `Block (default)`

Outbound connections: `Allow (default)`

Protected network connections: [Customize...]

Settings
Specify settings that control Windows Firewall behavior. [Customize...]

Logging
Specify logging settings for troubleshooting. [Customize...]

Learn more about these settings

[OK] [Cancel] [Apply]

The default behavior for Windows Firewall is to track outbound connections and allow inbound responses to any established connections. However, this behavior assumes a one-to-one connection (one source going to one destination, or *unicast*). When a computer sends out a *multicast* (one source going to many destinations) or *broadcast* (one source going to every destination on a network) message, the unicast response from the various destination computers won't be allowed back to the source computer. Allowing unicast responses under Windows Firewall with Advanced Security temporarily permits unicast responses from any destination responding to a multicast or broadcast message, for up to four seconds.

Customize Logging Settings for the Private Profile

Name: \system32\LogFiles\Firewall\pfirewall.log   Browse...

Size limit (KB): 4,096

Log dropped packets: No (default)

Log successful connections: No (default)

Note: If you are configuring the log file name on Group Policy object, ensure that the Windows Firewall service account has write permissions to the folder containing the log file.

Default path for the log file is %systemroot%\system32\logfiles\firewall\pfirewall.log.

Learn more about logging

OK   Cancel

10. In the Customize Logging Settings for the Private Profile window, you can specify the location and name to save your firewall logs and limit the size of the logs. You can also specify whether Windows Firewall logs dropped packets and successful connections. By default, only blocked connections are logged to reduce the amount of data written to the logs, and it is normally not necessary to log dropped packets or successful connections. Make any changes desired and click OK.

Scanning Your Computer with Windows Defender

Stuff You Need to Know

Toolbox:

✓ Computer running Windows 7

Time Needed:
25 minutes

Windows Defender is configured by default to scan your computer daily and provide real-time protection (scan any program that attempts to install on your computer). To manually scan your computer, follow these steps. (Depending on the contents of your hard drive, a manual scan could take only a few minutes or much longer.)

1. Click the Start button and type **Defender** in the Search Programs and Files text box.

2. Click Windows Defender in the search results.

3. Windows Defender is launched.

4. Click Scan to scan your computer for spyware.

5. The results of the scan are displayed.

Changing Previous Actions (Allow/Quarantine) in Windows Defender

Stuff You Need to Know

Toolbox:

✔ Computer running Windows 7

✔ Administrator account

Time Needed:
5 minutes

It happens to all of us: You're intensely focused on some YouTube video or other important work when a window suddenly pops up telling you some program is trying to blah, blah, blah — "Do you want to allow it or block it?" You're way too busy to actually read what it is, let alone understand the security implications of the program that is trying to run, so you click Allow and go on your merry way. Later, when you realize that might not have been the best thing you've ever done, Windows Defender makes it easy to go back and see what you did, and make any necessary changes.

Warning: Spyware can be very nasty, and removing actual spyware usually isn't as easy as clicking Remove or Undo, even with Windows Defender. It's best to take the time to read those vexing pop-up windows, understand what the program is trying to do, and avoid allowing spyware to be installed on your computer in the first place. And now, back to reality.

1. Click the Start button and type **Defender** in the "Search Programs and Files text box.

2. Click Windows Defender in the search results.

3. Windows Defender is launched.

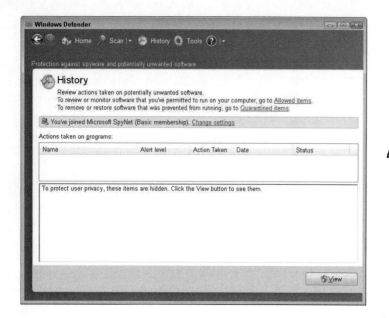

4. Click History to view the History screen.

5. To view all actions taken on programs, click the View button in the lower-right corner.

6. To clear your Windows Defender history, click the Clear History button in the lower-right corner.

7. Click Allowed Items, and then click the View button in the lower-right corner.

8. Any programs you have previously allowed will be displayed in the window. If you decide you no longer want to allow a program (or inadvertently clicked the option to allow a program when you were prompted), select the program and click the Remove from List button.

Clicking Remove from List does not automatically block the program — it just allows Windows Defender to rescan the program. You will need to deny the program access when prompted by Windows Defender.

9. Click the Back button (left arrow) in the upper-left corner to return to the previous window.

10. Click Quarantined Items, and then click the View button in the lower-right corner.

11. Any programs you have previously blocked will be displayed in the window. If you decide you want to allow a program (or inadvertently clicked the option to block a program when you were prompted), select the program and click the Restore button.

12. To permanently delete a program from your computer, select the program and click the Remove button. To permanently delete all quarantined programs from your computer, click the Remove All button.

After restoring a previously blocked program, you will still need to allow the program when prompted by Windows Defender.

Changing Microsoft SpyNet Settings

Stuff You Need to Know

Toolbox:
- ✔ Computer running Windows 7
- ✔ Administrator account

Time Needed:
5 minutes

Microsoft SpyNet is Microsoft's online community that helps them develop new spyware detection methods and improve Windows Defender's effectiveness. You should be aware that the information collected is automatically sent to Microsoft SpyNet (if you choose to participate), and that in some cases personal information may be inadvertently sent to Microsoft. But you can trust them — they're *not* from the government! And Microsoft promises not to use the collected information to identify you or contact you. There are three options for participating in Microsoft SpyNet: Basic (the default setting), Advanced (collects more detailed information about any spyware detected and how it affects your computer), and None. Follow these steps, to change your Microsoft SpyNet setting:

1. Click the Start button and type **Defender** in the Search Programs and Files text box.

2. Click Windows Defender in the search results.

3. Windows Defender is launched.

4. Click History to view the History screen.

5. Click Change Settings in the blue bar (midscreen) that states You've Joined Microsoft SpyNet.

6. Choose either Join with a Basic Membership, Join with an Advanced Membership, or I Don't Want to Join Microsoft SpyNet at This Time and click the Save button.

Configuring Tools and Settings in Windows Defender

Stuff You Need to Know

Toolbox:
- Computer running Windows 7
- Administrator account

Time Needed:
5 minutes

You can configure many advanced options in Windows Defender, such as automatic scanning, default actions, real-time protection settings, excluded files and folders, excluded file types, and more.

1. Click the Start button and type **Defender** in the Search Programs and Files text box.

2. Click Windows Defender in the search results.

3. Windows Defender is launched.

4. Click Tools to view the Tools and Settings screen.

5. Click Options under Settings.

6. Under Automatic Scanning, you can enable or disable automatic scanning, set the frequency (daily, or only on a specific day of the week), select the approximate time to start automatic scans, choose the type of scan (full or quick), check for updated definitions prior to scanning your computer, and choose to run the scan only when your compute is idle (so that performance will not be degraded while you're working on your computer). Click the Save button to apply your changes.

7. Under Default Actions, you can choose what action Windows Defender takes (Recommended Action Based on Definitions, Remove, Quarantine, or Allow) when a specific alert level (Severe, High, Medium, or Low) is triggered. The Recommended Action Based on Definitions setting enables Windows Defender to take advantage of the latest data (definitions) about Internet threats to take the most appropriate action. Click the Save button to apply your changes.

8. Under Real-time Protection, you can enable or disable real-time protection, choose whether to scan files and attachments that are downloaded via a Web browser, and choose whether to scan programs that are running on your computer (and may potentially allow spyware to run in the background). Real-time Protection allows Windows Defender to scan programs for spyware or other threats automatically as they are accessed on your computer or over the Internet.

9. Under Excluded Files and Folders, you can identify specific files or folders on your computer that you do not want Windows Defender to scan. You may choose to do this if Windows Defender causes a problem with certain files or folders. Click Add, and then browse to the directory location of the file or folder you wish to exclude and click OK. If you change your mind about excluding a file or folder, you can select it and click Remove. Click the Save button to apply your changes.

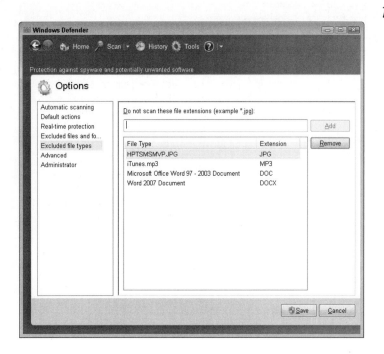

10. Under Excluded File Types, you can identify types of files that you do not want Windows Defender to scan, such as pictures (.jpg) or music (.mp3). You might exclude certain file types so that Windows Defender runs faster by skipping over your music files, for example. Although music and pictures are generally a low risk for spyware, it is not inconceivable that some vermin may attempt to disguise a malicious program as an innocent song or picture, so be careful if you do decide to exclude these files from scanning. Simply type the file extension — you don't need to include the asterisk (*) or leading period (.) and click Add. To scan any file types you have previously excluded, select the file type from the list and click Remove. Click the Save button to apply your changes.

11. Under Advanced, you can select whether to scan compressed files (for example, .zip files), e-mail and attachments, and removable drives (such as USB drives). You can also enable *heuristics,* which checks for partial matches of existing spyware definitions, and you can configure Windows Defender to automatically create a restore point before taking action on any detected items (so that you can recover your computer if the action causes a problem). Click the Save button to apply your changes.

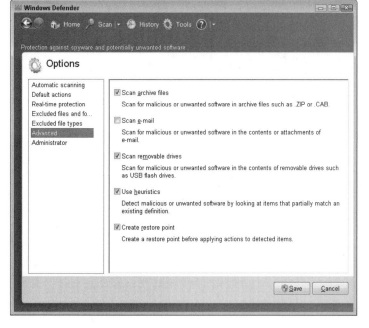

12. Under Administrator, you can select whether you want Windows Defender to alert all users when spyware is detected or only the administrator. You can also configure Windows Defender to allow the administrator to see the history, allowed items, and quarantined items for all users on the computer. Click the Save button to apply your changes.

Chapter 13

Windows Update

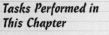

Tasks Performed in This Chapter

- ✔ Manually checking for updates
- ✔ Changing Windows Update settings
- ✔ Uninstalling updates
- ✔ Hiding updates and restoring hidden updates

Computer software and applications, including operating systems like Windows 7, are works in progress. If we had to wait for software vendors to perfect their programs, we wouldn't have any computer software! For this reason, bugs (and fixes) and security flaws (and patches) are a fact of life. Even when vendors put forth their best effort to build a stable and secure program, there are plenty of people in the world, with a variety of motivations (not always evil), that are looking for ways to break these programs. And, of course, when you're the biggest software vendor on the planet (Microsoft), you're easily the biggest target as well.

Windows Update is Microsoft's online portal for ensuring that software fixes and security patches are made available to the public, as soon as they are known and developed.

Windows updates are prioritized as

- ✔ **Important:** Improve security, privacy, and reliability.
- ✔ **Recommended:** Improve performance or address noncritical issues.
- ✔ **Optional:** Include new drivers or software to help improve performance or stability.

Different types of Windows updates include

- ✔ **Security update:** Fixes a known security vulnerability in a specific software product or version. These updates are further classified as critical, important, moderate, or low severity.
- ✔ **Critical update:** Fixes a critical, nonsecurity-related bug or a specific problem.
- ✔ **Service Pack:** A set of fixes and updates that have been tested and rolled up into a single installation.

Manually Checking for Updates

Although automatically checking for updates is the recommended setting, if you change Windows Update to never check for updates, you will need to periodically check for updates manually.

1. From the Control Panel, click System and Security.

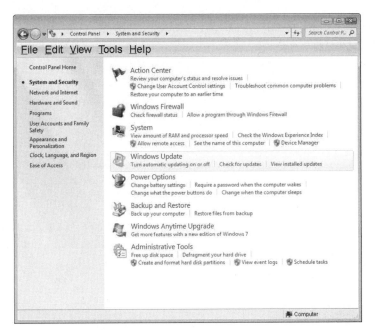

2. Click Windows Update.

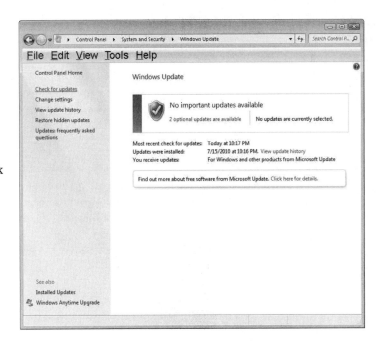

3. In the left pane, click Check for Updates.

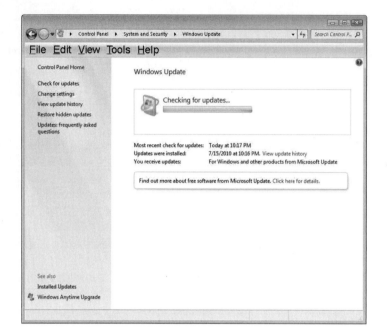

4. Windows connects to the Internet to check for updates.

5. After checking for updates, Windows Update reports any important or optional updates that were found. Click the link for any updates that you wish to install. (You see two optional updates in this example.)

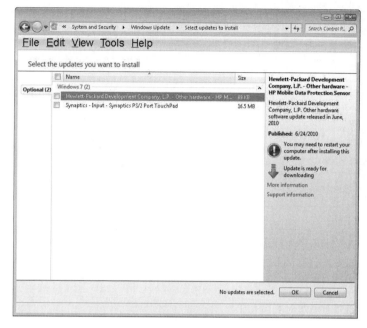

6. Select the updates that you want to install and click OK.

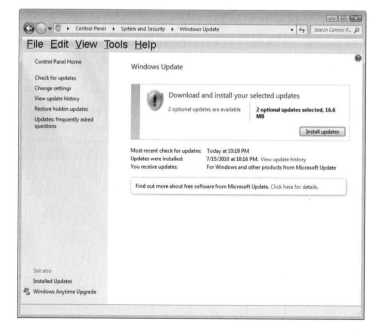

7. Click Install Updates.

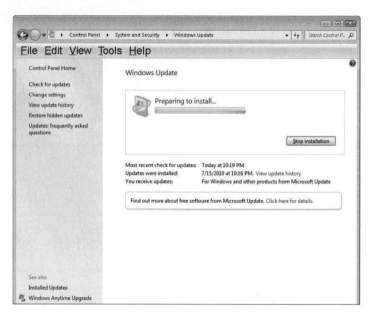

8. Windows downloads and installs the selected updates. You can stop the installation at any time by clicking Stop Installation.

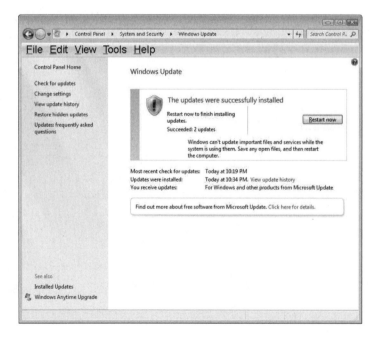

9. After the updates are downloaded and installed, Windows will prompt you if a restart is required. Click Restart Now.

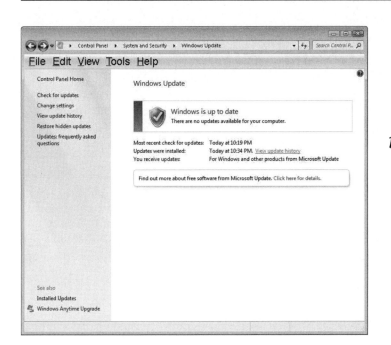

10. Click View Update History to see a log of all updates that have been applied to your computer. (If you had to restart your computer, follow Steps 1-3 to return to this screen.)

11. The log file is displayed showing the name of any updates installed, the status, importance, and date installed.

Changing Windows Update Settings

Stuff You Need to Know

Toolbox:

✔ Computer running Windows 7
✔ Administrator account

Time Needed:
5 minutes

There are several options for Windows Update that you can configure, such as how updates are downloaded and installed (automatically or manually) and who can install updates on your computer.

1. From the Control Panel, click System and Security.

2. Click Windows Update.

3. In the left pane, click Change Settings.

4. Under Important Updates, choose from one of the following four options in the drop-down menu: Install Updates Automatically (Recommended), Download Updates but Let Me Choose whether to Install Them, Check for Updates but Let Me Choose whether to Download and Install Them, or Never Check for Updates (Not Recommended).

5. If you select Install Updates Automatically, select how often to install new updates (daily or a specific day of the week) and at what time. These options are grayed out if you choose one of the other three options.

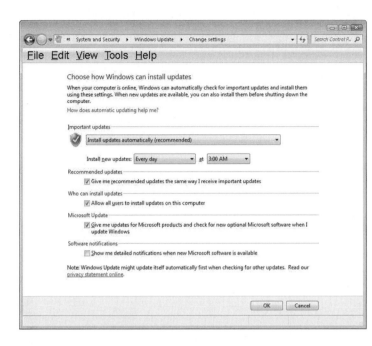

6. You can also select the following options:

Additional Windows Update Settings

Setting	*Description*
Recommended Updates	Select this check box if you want Windows Update to automatically install recommended updates as well as important updates.
Who Can Install Updates	Select this option to allow standard users to install updates. Otherwise, an administrator account is required.
Microsoft Update	This option checks for installed Microsoft products (such as Microsoft Office) and searches for updates to that software.
Software Notifications	Provides detailed information about new Microsoft software when it is available.

7. Click OK.

Removing Installed Updates

Stuff You Need to Know

Toolbox:

- ✔ Computer running Windows 7
- ✔ Administrator account

Time Needed:
5 minutes

Occasionally, an update causes problems on your computer. For example, an update may cause a program to not run correctly or to run much slower. To remove an installed update, follow these steps:

1. From the Control Panel, click Programs.

2. Under Programs and Features, click View Installed Updates.

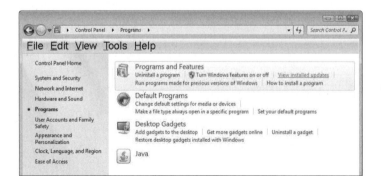

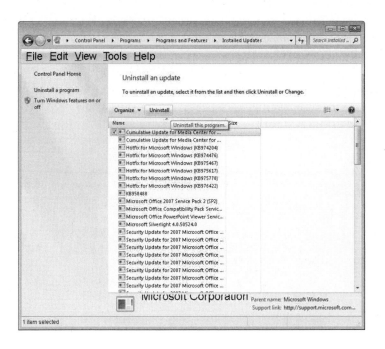

3. Select the update (or updates) you would like to uninstall. An Uninstall button will appear in the toolbar at the top (to the right of the Organize button). Click Uninstall.

4. Click Yes to confirm that you want to uninstall the update.

Hiding Updates

Stuff You Need to Know

Toolbox:

✓ Computer running Windows 7

✓ Administrator account

Time Needed:

5 minutes

After removing an installed update (see the previous task), Windows Update will constantly warn you that there are updates available. The solution to this problem is to hide the update.

1. From the Control Panel, click System and Security.

2. Click Windows Update.

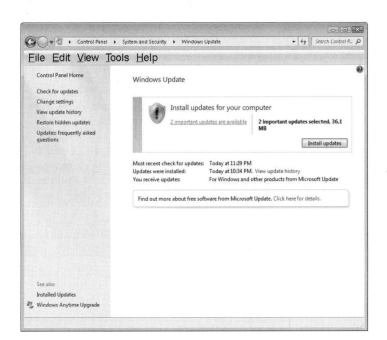

3. Click the link indicating that updates are available.

4. Right-click the update that you would like to hide and click Hide Update. Click OK.

Restoring Hidden Updates

Stuff You Need to Know

Toolbox:
- ✔ Computer running Windows 7
- ✔ Administrator account
- ✔ Internet connection

Time Needed:
5 minutes

At some point, you may install a newer version of a program that an update previously conflicted with, or some other configuration change may occur that makes the update and program compatible. At this point, you may want to restore the hidden update (or updates) and install them on your computer, particularly if the update is a security update or is otherwise listed as important. As part of the restore process, Windows will check to see if there is a more current update available, which may supersede the previous update altogether. To restore hidden updates, follow these steps.

1. From the Control Panel, click System and Security.

2. Click Windows Update.

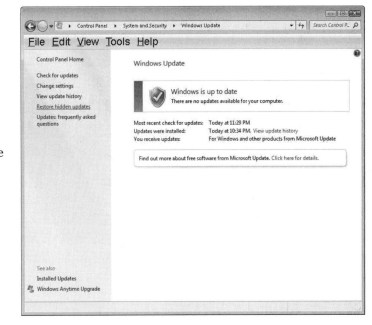

3. In the left pane, click Restore Hidden Updates.

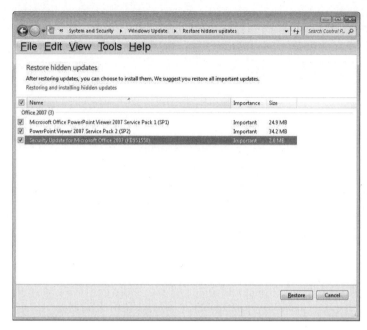

4. Select the updates you would like to restore and click Restore.

5. Windows will automatically check for new updates.

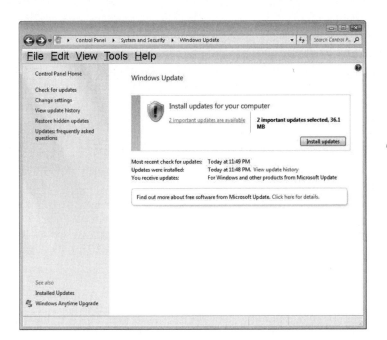

6. Before installing the updates, verify that they are the correct updates that you want to install by clicking the link indicating that updates are available.

7. Select the updates you wish to install and click OK.

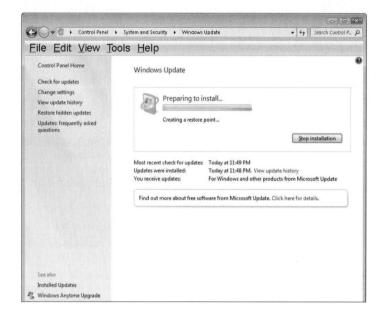

8. Windows Update downloads and installs the selected updates.

9. Windows Update indicates the status of the installation (for example, Succeeded, Failed, or Not Needed).

Chapter 14

Backup and Restore

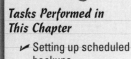

Tasks Performed in This Chapter

- ✔ Setting up scheduled backups
- ✔ Managing backups
- ✔ Restoring files
- ✔ Disabling and enabling the backup schedule
- ✔ Creating a system image
- ✔ Creating a system repair disc
- ✔ Restoring a system image

On a corporate network, data on servers is regularly backed up and retained according to an established backup retention policy. Third-party backup software is used to ensure that timely, accurate, and secure backups are created and maintained. Backup hardware may consist of large disk-based systems, tape drives and libraries, or a combination of these technologies, and the backed-up data is either stored off-site in a secure facility or replicated to a remote location. About the only time the subject of backups ever comes up is when someone frantically calls his IT department because he has inadvertently deleted an important document or spreadsheet. And like magic, the file is restored, and at worst, only a few hours of work have been lost.

On your home network, you alone are responsible for backing up your data, keeping it safe, managing it, and restoring files when something goes wrong! Unfortunately, regularly backing up your computer and data is one of those things that far too many people talk about, but never actually do. Fortunately, Windows 7 makes it easy to automate this important task so that you can (relatively) easily recover from a hard drive crash, computer virus, corrupted file, or a trigger-happy finger on the Delete key!

Determining Where to Save Your Backup

You can save your backups on several different types of media using Windows Backup. These include hard drives, writeable CDs or DVDs, USB flash drives, and network shares. The advantages and disadvantages of each type are explained in the sections that follow.

Hard drives (internal or external)

Here are the advantages to using hard drives for saving your backup:

▎ ✔ **Large capacity:** Hard drives have the largest capacity of all the possible backup media choices in Windows Backup.

✔ **Relatively inexpensive:** The cost per gigabyte of storage space is low, compared to other storage media such as CDs or DVDs.

✔ **Portability (external only):** External hard drives are fairly portable and many can be easily connected to your computer via a USB port.

✔ **Speedy:** Internal hard drives are more efficient than external hard drives or flash drives that connect to the computer via a USB port, and both types of hard drive are more efficient than writeable CD/DVD drives.

The disadvantages for using hard drives include:

✔ **Difficult to install (internal):** An internal hard drive can be difficult to install.

✔ **Susceptible to damage:** A hard drive, unlike your other storage options, has moving parts — very fast moving parts — which are susceptible to physical damage (particularly external hard drives) and crashes.

✔ **Not portable (internal only):** Regularly removing an internal hard drive to store it in a fireproof safe or other secure location isn't practical.

Writeable CDs or DVDs

Advantages of using writeable CDs or DVDs to save your backup are:

✔ **Convenience:** You can buy CD-R/RW and DVD-R/RW discs just about anywhere.

✔ **Cost:** CDs and DVDs are relatively inexpensive.

✔ **Portability:** CDs and DVDs can be easily transported and stored in a secure location, such as a fireproof safe.

✔ **Durability:** Although they are not indestructible, CDs and DVDs do not have any moving parts, and are less susceptible to physical damage than hard drives, including water damage.

Disadvantages of using writeable CDs or DVDs are as follows:

✔ **No scheduled system images:** You can't save a scheduled system image backup to a CD or DVD.

✔ **Limited capacity:** CDs and DVDs have relatively limited capacity, meaning it may take numerous discs to do a backup. You'll need to store all of those discs and label them correctly in order to keep track of them.

✔ **Can't erase and can only write once:** You can't erase a CD-R or DVD-R and you can burn data to it only once. After you've written data to it, it's there forever. You have to destroy the disc to get rid of the data, and you'll eventually end up with a large (and perhaps unmanageable) stack of discs. CD-RW and DVD-RW discs do not have these limitations.

USB flash drives

The advantages of using USB flash drives for saving your backup include:

- ✔ **Convenience:** You can buy USB flash drives just about anywhere.

- ✔ **Cost:** USB flash drives are relatively inexpensive.

- ✔ **Portability:** USB flash drives can be easily transported and stored in a secure location, such as a fireproof safe.

- ✔ **Relatively durable:** Although they are not indestructible, USB flash drives do not have any moving parts and are less susceptible to physical damage than hard drives or CDs and DVDs.

The disadvantages for using a USB flash drive are:

- ✔ **No system images:** You can't save a system image on a USB flash drive.

- ✔ **Easily lost:** USB flash drives may be *too* compact and convenient for some people. Because of their small size, USB flash drives can be easily lost . . . or perhaps left in a pocket and run through the laundry!

- ✔ **Limited capacity:** Although storage capacities are increasing, USB flash drives still have relatively limited capacity and are more expensive per gigabyte than other storage options.

Network shares

A network share is just a hard drive located on your network, so it has all the same advantages and disadvantages as a computer hard drive.

In addition to the same disadvantages as a hard drive, network shares have the following disadvantages:

- ✔ **Version support:** You can save your backup to a network location only if you are using Windows 7 Professional, Ultimate, or Enterprise.

- ✔ **Security:** Other people who have access to the network location may also have access to your backups.

- ✔ **Most recent system image only:** When you create a system image on a network share, Windows keeps only the most recent version.

Another option for backing up your critical data is to forgo Windows Backup altogether and instead use an online backup service for a small monthly fee, such as Carbonite (www.carbonite.com), Mozy (www.mozy.com), or iDrive (www.idrive.com).

Setting Up Backups

Stuff You Need to Know

Toolbox:

- ✔ Computer running Windows 7
- ✔ Administrator account
- ✔ A writeable CD or DVD drive (optional)
- ✔ Several blank CD-R/RW or DVD-R/RW discs, a hard drive (internal, external, or shared network), or a USB drive

Time Needed:

15 minutes

Once you've figured out exactly what you want to back up, how often you want to back it up, and what you're going to back it up onto (see the sidebar "Where should I save my backup?"), it's time to set it up!

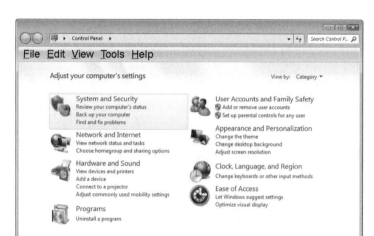

1. From the Control Panel, click System and Security.

2. Under Backup and Restore, click Back up Your Computer.

3. Under Backup, click Set up Backup.

4. Windows 7 detects any hard disks or removable drives installed on your computer. The Select Where You Want to Save Your Backup screen appears. Select a destination for your backups and click Next and move on to Step 7.

5. Alternatively, you can click Save on a Network to save your backups to a shared location on your network. The Select a Network Location window opens. Enter the network location manually in the format *server**share*, where *server* is the name of the computer that you will be saving your backups onto and *share* is the folder on that computer. You can also click Browse to navigate directly to the computer and folder destination for your backups.

WARNING! If the destination device that you select does not support security permissions (which is likely), a warning will appear indicating that other people may be able to access your backup data if they have physical access to the destination device. You should store your backups in a secure place (such as a lockable fireproof cabinet, a personal safe, or a bank safe deposit box).

TIP The network location must be available at the time the backup is scheduled to run, so if you set up your backups to run at 2 a.m., be sure the source computer and the destination computer with the network drive are both on.

6. Under Network Credentials, enter a username and password that Windows Backup can use to access the network location.

7. Next, select what you want to back up. If you select Let Windows Choose, the libraries (Documents, Music, Pictures, and Videos), as well as any files saved on the desktop and in any default Windows folders, are backed up for all users on the computer. (Go to Step 9.) If you select Let Me Choose, you will be able to designate what gets backed up on your computer. Click Next.

8. To select the folders that you want to back up, select the check box to the left of the folder. You can click the arrow to the left of the check box to expand the directory further, and then select or deselect subdirectories. You can also select the check box to create a system image if your backup destination device supports backup images. (See the "Creating a System Image" task later in this chapter.) Click Next.

If you can access the network location from the Computer folder on your computer without having to type a username and password, the account you are logged in with has the correct permissions to perform a backup to the network location. Use that username and password in the dialog box. Otherwise, you will need to enter the username and password for an account that is set up on the destination computer (or server).

If other people on your network have access to the network location you specify for your backups, they may be able to access your backups.

Set up backup

Review your backup settings

Backup Location: Removable Disk (I:)

Backup Summary:

Items	Included in backup
All users	Default Windows folders and lo...

Schedule: Every Sunday at 7:00 PM Change schedule

Save settings and run backup   Cancel

9. On the Review Your Backup Settings screen under Schedule, click the Change Schedule link.

Set up backup

How often do you want to back up?

Files that have changed and new files that have been created since your last backup will be added to your backup according to the schedule you set below.

☑ Run backup on a schedule (recommended)

How often: Weekly

What day: Sunday

What time: 7:00 PM

OK   Cancel

10. Under How Often Do You Want to Back Up?, you can disable scheduled backups (not recommended) and choose how often (daily, weekly, monthly), what day of the week or month (1 through 31, or the last day of the month), and at what time you want your backups to run. Click OK.

Set up backup

Review your backup settings

Backup Location: Removable Disk (I:)

Backup Summary:

Items	Included in backup
All users	Default Windows folders and lo...

Schedule: Every Sunday at 7:00 PM Change schedule

Save settings and run backup   Cancel

11. Click Save Settings and Run Backup.

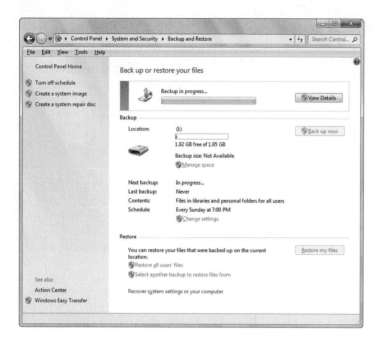

12. Windows Backup begins your first backup. You can click View Details to see more information about your backup or stop the backup.

13. Click Stop Backup to discontinue the backup job, for example, if the backup job is taking too long and therefore slowing down your computer, or if you realize you've made a mistake selecting what needs to be backed up.

14. When Windows Backup is ready to begin writing your backup job to the backup location, it will verify that the destination is available (for example, a blank DVD-R disk or USB drive). If not, you will be prompted to insert the correct media for the backup job. Windows will also instruct you to label the blank media and recommends a label. You don't have to use the exact label that Windows recommends (which consists of the computer name, date and time, and the drive or disk number). You might instead label it with something that is more meaningful to you, such as "My Documents, full backup, January 25, 2011."

Back Up Files

Label and insert a blank media

Please write the following label on a blank media and insert it into I:\

OWNER-PC 8/14/2010 5:42 PM Drive 1

OK   Stop backup

Windows Backup...100% complete

Windows Backup has completed successfully

Finished

Open the Backup and Restore Control Panel to view settings

Close

15. When your backup has successfully completed, Windows Backup will indicate the status. Click Close.

Managing Backups

Windows Backup is great for scheduling automatic backups to help ensure your important files are regularly backed up. Unfortunately, it doesn't have an automated process for deleting old backups. You still need to do this bit of housekeeping manually. If you don't, your old backups will eventually grow out of control. If you're backing up to a writeable CD or DVD, deleting your backups is as easy as *destroying* the disk. Otherwise, use Windows Backup to manually prune old backup jobs from your hard drive, USB flash drive, or network share.

Warning: Be sure to actually destroy any CDs or DVDs containing your backups. Simply throwing them away potentially exposes your private data to dumpster-diving thieves.

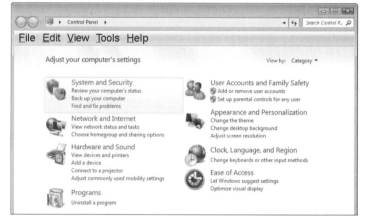

1. From the Control Panel, click System and Security.

2. Under Backup and Restore, click Back up Your Computer.

3. Under Backup, click Manage Space.

4. In the Manage Windows Backup Disk Space window under Data File Backup, click View backups.

5. Select the backup period you wish to delete, and then click the Delete button.

6. A Warning pops up asking if you really want to delete the selected backup. Click Delete and Run Backup Now.

7. Windows Backup deletes the selected backups. Click Close when the process is completed.

Windows Backup backs up only those files that have changed since your last backup. When a file is backed up, the File Is Ready for Archiving file attribute is deselected. (You can verify this by right-clicking any file and selecting Properties, then clicking the Advanced button under Attributes.) When you make a change to a file, this file attribute is automatically selected, which tells Windows Backup that the file needs to be backed up the next time Windows Backup runs. If you delete an old backup, any files that were contained in that backup will have the archiving file attribute selected again unless a more recent backup of those files exists (for example, if you modified any of the files after the backup you are deleting and have since run Windows Backup). However, it is very likely there will be files that haven't changed since the backup you are deleting, and therefore no backup copy will exist of those files. For this reason, you should choose the option to Delete and Run Backup Now (in Step 6) to ensure you get a good backup of all your files as quickly as possible.

8. In the Manage Windows Backup Disk Space window, click Close.

9. A new backup begins automatically.

Restoring Files from a Backup

Stuff You Need to Know

Toolbox:
- ✔ Computer running Windows 7
- ✔ Administrator account
- ✔ Your backup device or discs

Time Needed:
15 minutes

When that dreaded day comes (no, not *that* dreaded day!) and you discover that you've accidentally deleted your iTunes library or a virus has wreaked havoc on your files, you can relax. Breathe calmly and evenly, and follow these steps to restore your files from a backup.

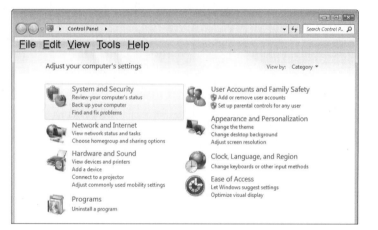

1. From the Control Panel, click System and Security.

2. Under Backup and Restore, click Restore Files from Backup.

3. Under Restore, click Restore My Files.

4. In the Restore Files window, you can either search for a file or folder to restore by name, or you can browse for files or folders to restore.

5. By default, Windows Backup will restore the files and folders that you select from the most recent backup. If you want to restore an older file or folder version (for example, you realize you accidentally deleted something from a file yesterday, then backed it up last night, and therefore you need to restore an older version of the file, possibly from a backup 2 days ago), click Choose a Different Date. A dialog box showing all of the available backups appears. You can choose which backups to view from the drop-down menu: Last Week, Last 1 Month, Last 6 Months, Last 12 Months, or All. Select the desired backup and click OK.

6. If you click Search in Step 4, the Search for Files to Restore dialog box appears. You can type in all or part of a filename or folder, or the file type (for example, `.docx`, `.xlsx`, `.jpg`, `.mp3`). Click the Search button. Select the files or folders that you want to restore (you can also click the Select All or Clear All button) by selecting the check box to the left of your highlighted selection, and click OK.

7. If you click Browse for Files in Step 4, the Browse the Backup for Files dialog box appears. Navigate to the file or files that you want to restore and select them by selecting the check box to the left of your highlighted selection. Click Add Files.

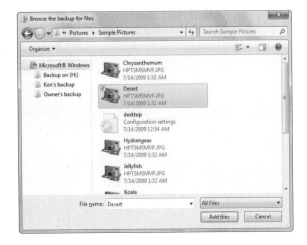

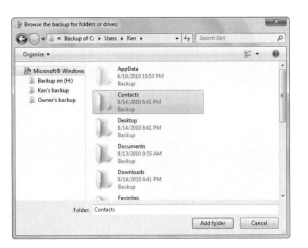

8. If you click Browse for Folders, the Browse the Backup for Folders or Drives dialog box appears. Navigate to the folder or drive that you want to restore, highlight it, and click Add Folder.

9. Click Next.

10. You can restore your files to the original location, or to an alternative location. To restore to an alternative location, click In the Following Location and click the Browse button.

In most cases, you should always restore to a location other than the original location in order to avoid accidentally overwriting a good copy of a file or folder.

11. Browse to the desired destination folder, or highlight a drive or directory and click Make New Folder. For example, select Local Disk (C:) and click Make New Folder. A new folder appears in the directory. Name the folder Restored Files. Click OK.

12. Click Restore the Files to Their Original Subfolders to keep the same folder structure as the original, in the new location. Click Restore.

13. Windows Backup restores your files and folders to the desired location. Click the View Restored Files link to go directly to the directory where your files were restored. Click Finish.

Turning the Backup Schedule Off and On

Stuff You Need to Know

Toolbox:
- Computer running Windows 7
- Administrator account

Time Needed:
5 minutes

To temporarily disable (or re-enable) your backup schedule, follow these steps:

1. From the Control Panel, click System and Security.

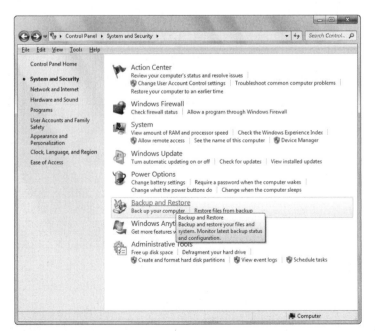

2. Click Backup and Restore.

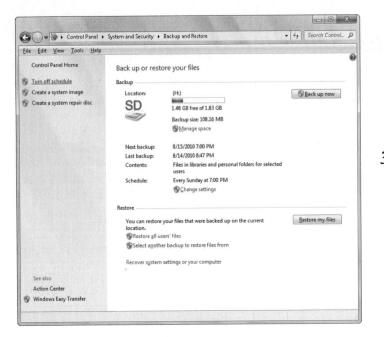

3. In the left pane, click Turn Off Schedule.

4. To turn the schedule back on, click Turn On Schedule under Backup on the Backup and Restore screen.

Creating a System Image

Stuff You Need to Know

Toolbox:

- Computer running Windows 7
- Administrator account
- A writeable CD or DVD drive
- Several blank CD-R/RW or DVD-R/RW discs

Time Needed:

1 hour

Having a backup of all your important files and folders is great, but what happens to all of your programs when your hard drive crashes or a virus wipes everything out? Reinstalling Windows 7 and all of your programs can be a very daunting — and a time-consuming task. And don't forget, you still have to install all of the updates and patches, configure your custom tweaks and settings, and restore all of your data! A system image creates a snapshot in time of your hard drive and can be a real life-saver — well, at least a time-saver — when a hard drive crashes.

Tip: If you have the disk space available on your backup device (for example, an external hard drive), Windows Backup can create a system image for you each time your regular backup runs. However, it isn't necessary to create system images as frequently as you back up your data. As a general guideline, you should create a new system image when you install any new programs or make major changes or updates to your computer or Windows 7. You should also create a new system image every few months — just to be safe!

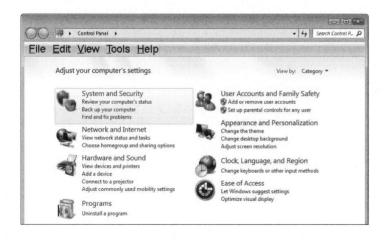

1. From the Control Panel, click System and Security.

2. Click Backup and Restore.

3. In the left pane, click Create a System Image.

4. Windows Backup scans your computer for backup devices.

5. You can create a system image on an NTFS-formatted hard disk (but not the same hard disk that you are creating the image from), on one or more discs, or to a network location. If you create a system image in a network location, Windows Backup overwrites older system images and keeps only the most recent image. Click Next.

Create a system image

Confirm your backup settings

Backup location:

DVD RW Drive (F:)

The backup could take up to 89 GB of disk space.

The following drives will be backed up:

SYSTEM (System)

(C:) (System)

RECOVERY (D:) (System)

Start backup | Cancel

Create a system image

Where do you want to save the backup?

A system image is a copy of the drives required for Windows to run. It can also include additional drives. A system image can be used to restore your computer if your hard drive or computer ever stops working; however, you can't choose individual items to restore. How do I restore my computer from a system image?

○ On a hard disk

SD Card (H:) 1.48 GB free

● On one or more DVDs

DVD RW Drive (F:)

○ On a network location

Select...

Next | Cancel

6. Confirm your backup destination is correct and click Start Backup.

Create a system image

Label and insert a blank media bigger than 1GB

Please write the following label on a blank media and insert it into F:

OWNER-PC 8/15/2010 10:25 AM 1

OK | Stop backup

7. Windows Backup starts creating your system image. You will be prompted to insert blank discs (if you're backing up to DVDs) when needed.

DVD-R/RWs are a good choice for creating system images; they're durable, inexpensive, and easy to use — both for creating and restoring a system image.

Before you can use a hard disk, you have to format it. There are two commonly used formats in Windows: FAT32 and NTFS. NTFS supports security permissions on directories and is the default file system used in Windows 7. To verify your drive format, open Computer from your desktop and right-click the drive letter (for example, C:). On the General tab near the top, you will see the type of disk (for example, Local Disk) and the file system (for example, NTFS or FAT32).

Creating a System Repair Disk

You can use a system repair disk to boot your computer when all else fails. It is one of several recovery tools you may need in order to restore your computer. A system repair disk can be used if there is any hope at all of saving your files. You can think of it as a car collision repair shop. You use it when there is damage that can hopefully be repaired. But if your car, umm computer, is a total loss, you'll need to restore a system image, which I explain in the next task.

Tip: Your PC manufacturer most likely included its branded version of a system recovery disk with your computer, and you can also use your Windows 7 DVD to boot your computer. Having a system repair disk provides additional insurance in case you encounter problems with the other recovery tools.

1. From the Control Panel, click System and Security.

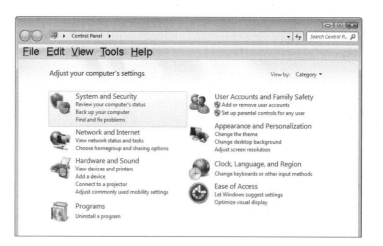

2. Click Backup and Restore.

3. In the left pane, click Create a System Repair Disc.

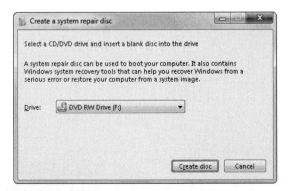

4. Select the writeable CD/DVD drive that will be used to create the system repair disc (if you have more than one writeable CD or DVD drive in your computer), insert a blank disc, and click Create Disc.

Restoring a System Image

Stuff You Need to Know

Toolbox:
- ✔ Computer running Windows 7
- ✔ Administrator account
- ✔ A writeable CD or DVD drive
- ✔ Several blank CD-R/RW or DVD-R/RW discs

Time Needed:
1 hour

Your hard drive has crashed and all is lost. It's a hopeless situation — well, not quite. You've got a system image! To restore your computer from a system image, follow these steps.

Warning: When you restore from a system image, you will reformat your hard drive and lose everything! Of course, if your hard drive is truly toast, your data is already gone, and restoring from an image is your last resort. Fortunately, in addition to your system image, you've got recent backups of all your files, right?

1. Insert your Windows 7 DVD and restart your computer. When the Welcome screen appears, click Repair Your Computer. Alternatively, you can boot your computer using your system repair disc, choose Repair Your Computer on the Advanced Boot Options screen, and press Enter.

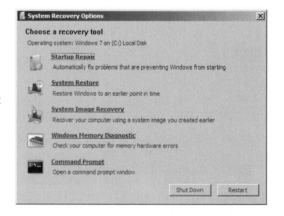

2. In the System Recovery Options window, select System Image Recovery and click Restart.

3. When prompted, insert your system image disc.

Chapter 15

Building a SOHO Network

Rapid technological innovations over the past decade have made SOHO (small office/home office) networks a commonplace reality for many people who enjoy the benefits of telecommuting, teleworking, or running a home-based business. Telecommuting and teleworking are no longer limited to a few privileged executives working from a home office, and home-based businesses are no longer limited to low-paying, menial start-up businesses, such as stuffing envelopes. Examples of some of the technological innovations that have made this possible include

✔ High-speed Internet (See Chapter 8.)

✔ Wi-Fi (Find out all about Wi-Fi technology in Chapter 4.)

✔ Virtual private networks, also known as VPNs (See Chapter 9.)

✔ Voice-over-IP (VoIP) phones

Teleworking is a relatively new trend in the workplace. It is distinctly different from telecommuting, which is more or less simply defined as working from home. Teleworking is independent of your location, and can be done from your home, a hotel room, a client's office, a train, an airport, a car (with someone else driving), or just about anywhere.

In this chapter, I tell you about some of the special considerations that you need to be aware of if you're setting up a SOHO network.

Recognizing the Benefits of Working from Home

Sure, you understand the benefits of working from home from your perspective! But what's in it for your employer? Here are a few benefits you can espouse to help you make your case:

✔ **Cost reductions:** Small businesses spend approximately $5,000 per employee, per year for facilities costs that include things such as leased space, utilities, furniture, and office equipment and supplies.

✔ **Increased productivity:** Several studies have shown that many people are actually more productive working from home rather than working in an office. Even if your employer won't buy into the "a happy employee is a productive employee" mantra, there are practical reasons why working from home can improve productivity, such as not losing time to daily commutes, working during inclement weather, working when you're a little under the weather, and not getting your coworkers sick when you come into the office sneezing and wheezing (a phenomenon known as presenteeism).

✔ **Boosted morale:** Flexible working arrangements can be an important benefit to many employees. In fact, some studies show that a flexible work schedule, which might include working from home, is more important to many employees than a higher salary.

✔ **Going green:** To quote the famous philosopher Kermit the Frog, "It isn't easy being green!" With so many businesses looking for green initiatives today, here's an easy one: A typical employee's commute contributes about 5,000 pounds of harmful carbon emissions to the environment each year and uses about 400 gallons of fuel. To put that in context, you would need to plant 12 trees a year to offset 5,000 pounds of carbon emissions. Allowing an employee to work from home just one day a week can reduce carbon emissions by more than 1,000 pounds and gas consumption by 78 gallons a year.

Location, Location, Location

Whether you're running your own home business or teleworking from a home office, location is every bit as important as it is to a traditional bricks-and-mortar business, but for different reasons. Part of the appeal of a home network is that you can use your computers, printers, and other network gadgets from practically any room in your house, particularly if you've gone the wireless route. (See Chapter 4.) But it's important to establish boundaries between your personal and work life, for several reasons:

✔ **Practicality:** It can be very distracting or embarrassing to have a conference call while your dog is barking, your infant son is crying, or your television is blaring SpongeBob SquarePants in the background.

✔ **Tax benefits:** You may be able to take several tax deductions for your home office, including the portion of your home that you designate as your office or place of business, as well as any computers, phones, Internet access, and other equipment or expenses related to your home office.

✔ **Sanity:** Just because you can sit up in your bed and technically be at work when you have a home office doesn't mean you should! In fact, you shouldn't. When you're working from home, it is important to establish a daily work routine that includes getting out of bed, getting dressed, and "going to work" in your home office. Your family, roommates, pets, and others should understand that you are at work — you just happen to have a really short commute!

Tax laws are constantly changing. You should consult an accountant or tax attorney to get the most accurate information about the tax benefits of your home office or home business.

Regulatory Compliance

Believe it or not, when you're running a home business or working from home, there are various regulations in effect that may require you to take some additional security measures on your home network. A few that may apply to your particular home business or work industry include PCI, HIPAA, and various state disclosure laws.

Payment Card Industry Data Security Standards (PCI DSS)

PCI DSS (commonly referred to as simply PCI) applies to any business, regardless of size, that processes credit or debit card transactions. Although PCI is not a legal requirement (yet), if your business fails to comply, you can lose your authorization to accept major credit and debit cards such as MasterCard, Visa, and American Express, making it next to impossible to conduct business over the Internet, or even in person in our increasingly noncash world of commerce. Minor violations of PCI can cost you fines of up to $25,000 per month, and an actual loss or theft of financial data resulting from noncompliance can cost you as much as $500,000!

Whether your home or small business handles thousands of credit card transactions every week, or only a single transaction a year, PCI compliance is a must.

If your home or small business handles thousands of credit card transactions every week, the do-it-yourself route may not be the best route for building and securing your network!

PCI consists of 12 core requirements (which I've summarized in Table 15-1) and over 200 specific security controls. You can download the complete and official PCI specification, as well as other useful tools and information, at `www.pcisecurity standards.org`.

Table 15-1	Summary of PCI Requirements
Requirement 1	Install and maintain a firewall configuration to protect cardholder data.
Requirement 2	Do not use vendor-supplied defaults for any system passwords and other security parameters.
Requirement 3	Protect stored cardholder data.
Requirement 4	Encrypt transmission of cardholder data across open, public networks.
Requirement 5	Use and regularly update antivirus software.
Requirement 6	Develop and maintain secure systems and applications.
Requirement 7	Restrict a person's access to cardholder data by business need to know.
Requirement 8	Assign a unique ID to each person with computer access.

(continued)

Table 15-1 *(continued)*	
Requirement 9	Restrict physical access to cardholder data.
Requirement 10	Track and monitor all access to network resources and cardholder data.
Requirement 11	Regularly test security systems and processes.
Requirement 12	Maintain a policy that addresses information security.

Health care

With the recent changes and rapid expansion of the U.S. health care system (and other health care systems throughout the world), there are many new opportunities for small and home-based businesses, for example in electronic medical records (EMRs) and elderly care. If your work or business involves health care, there's a good chance that the Health Insurance Portability and Accountability Act (HIPAA) and the Health Information Technology for Economic and Clinical Health Act (HITECH) may have an impact on how you conduct business on your SOHO network. Both acts are intended to protect the privacy and security of individual health information, known as protected health information (PHI).

Specific HIPAA and HITECH requirements can be found on the U.S. Department of Health & Human Services Web site at www.hhs.gov.

State privacy and disclosure laws

Many states have enacted data privacy and disclosure laws that require a business to protect private information and to notify individuals when personal data has been lost, stolen, or otherwise compromised. These laws are often applicable to any person or business that has customers in the state, or that stores or processes personal data about a citizen of the state. A total of 46 U.S. states, Washington D.C., Puerto Rico, and the U.S. Virgin Islands have data security and public disclosure laws.

Many regulations, such as the HITECH Act and various state privacy and disclosure laws, provide *safe harbor* (an exception) if you encrypt your data (discussed in the next section).

Data Confidentiality and Encryption

Protecting the confidentiality of the data stored on your network becomes significantly more important when you're running a home business or working from home. Threats such as viruses, worms, Trojan horses, and other malware (see Chapter 12) are bad enough when they destroy or steal your personal data. But when corporate data or your customers' personal data is stolen or destroyed, you've got a much bigger problem. In addition to protecting this data from Internet threats, it's important to keep it safe with user accounts and permissions (see

Chapter 5) to avoid someone else on your home network accidentally deleting your work, and to regularly back it all up (see Chapter 14) — just in case!

Encryption converts data, such as a document or spreadsheet, into an unintelligible, scrambled format, to protect the confidentiality of the data. Encryption protects data by making it unreadable until it is *decrypted*, or unscrambled, using the correct cipher and key.

Encryption is also used to protect the integrity of data and verify its authenticity. These advanced encryption topics are beyond the scope of this book.

A *cipher* is a mathematical algorithm used to scramble data. In cryptography, there are known ciphers and, much less commonly, restricted ciphers. A known cipher is preferable because it relies on its mathematical complexity and the strength of the key (essentially a password or digital certificate) to protect data. A restricted cipher relies on the secrecy of the mathematical formula, rather than its complexity, to protect data. This may seem counterintuitive, but it actually makes sense if you consider the following two examples.

A deadbolt lock can be easily identified, and its inner working mechanisms aren't closely guarded state secrets. What makes a deadbolt lock effective is the individual key that controls a specific lock on a specific door. If the key is weak (imagine only one or two notches on a flat key) or not well protected (left under your doormat), the lock won't protect your belongings. Similarly, if a hacker or thief is able to determine what encryption algorithm (lock) was used to encrypt your data, it should still be safe because you're using a strong key (complex password) that you've kept secret, rather than a cute a little password (like your dog's name) that you've taped to your keyboard!

On the other hand, a lock that no one has ever seen before may initially keep out intruders, but eventually someone will discover how the lock works — especially if it's installed on millions of doors — and the lock will no longer be effective, particularly if the inner workings of the lock are relatively simple. Just think about how difficult it is to keep a secret between a few people, let alone among millions of consumers (notwithstanding the secret formula for Coca-Cola or KFC!).

The two most commonly used encryption standards today are 3DES (Triple Data Encryption Standard; pronounced *triple-des*) and AES (Advanced Encryption Standard).

The Encrypting File System (EFS) is a Windows program that encrypts individual files and folders on your hard disk. EFS is available in Windows 7 Professional Edition and Ultimate Edition. BitLocker is a complementary (as in, it goes with EFS — not that it's free!) program that works with EFS and is used to encrypt the entire hard disk. BitLocker is available in Windows 7 Ultimate and Enterprise Editions only.

EFS is a program that runs after Windows starts. This means that it is potentially vulnerable to programs that exploit weaknesses in the Windows operating system. There are many well-known vulnerabilities and widely available programs built specifically to crack an EFS-encrypted hard drive.

BitLocker runs before Windows starts. It protects your hard disk contents from Windows vulnerabilities by encrypting everything on your hard disk, including Windows.

A few important things to know about EFS include the following:

- ✔ You can't encrypt certain files or folders, such as system files and anything in the Windows folder.

- ✔ You can't encrypt any files or folders that aren't on an NTFS (NT File System) partition. You can check this by right-clicking your hard disk (for example, C:) in Windows Explorer and looking at the file system. (See Figure 15-1.)

- ✔ You can't encrypt a Windows-compressed file or folder. But you can encrypt a file or folder compressed with a third-party program such as WinZip. You can also decompress a file or folder, and then encrypt it.

- ✔ Windows 7 automatically decrypts a file (and will not automatically re-encrypt it) when you send it via e-mail, copy it to a different network location, or save it onto a hard disk partition that is not an NTFS partition.

- ✔ EFS doesn't prevent someone from accidentally (or maliciously) deleting an encrypted file.

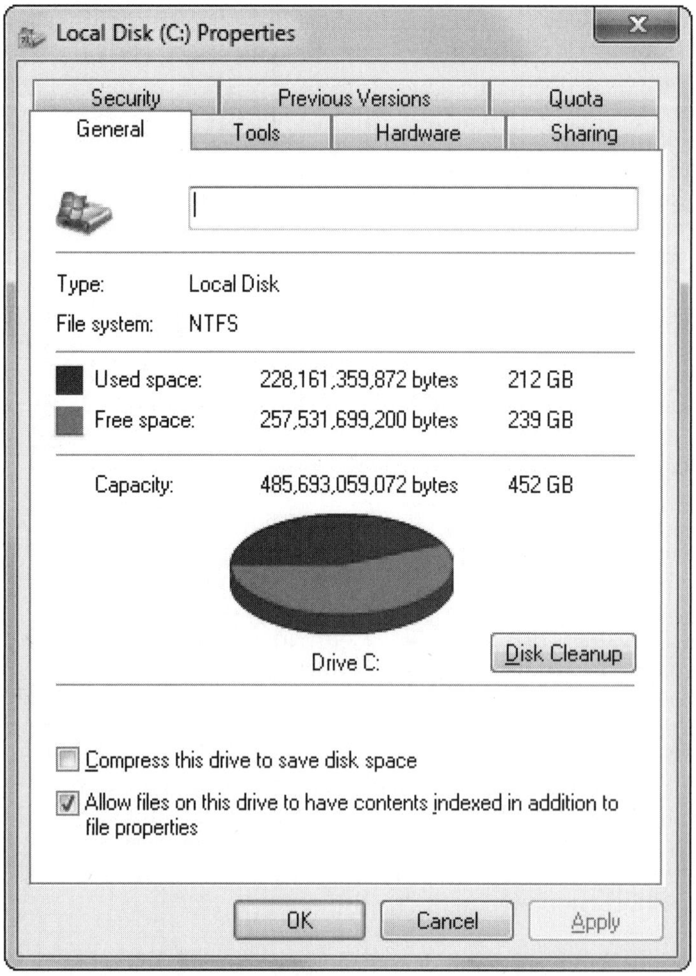

Figure 15-1: Checking the file system type.

NT (as in *new technology*) was the original name of the Windows version that was made for business use (Windows NT 3.5, 3.51, and 4.0). Later versions (such as Windows 2000, Windows 2003, and Windows 2008) dropped the NT designation, but many of the technologies, concepts, and terms remain.

Windows 7 Ultimate Edition also includes BitLocker To Go, which encrypts removal media, such as USB drives.

There are many excellent, inexpensive (less expensive than upgrading from Windows 7 Professional Edition to Windows 7 Ultimate Edition), and easy-to-use third-party disk encryption programs available from security vendors such as McAfee (www.mcafee.com) and Sophos (www.sophos.com).

Setting up Encrypting File System (EFS)

Stuff You Need to Know

Toolbox:

☑ Computer running Windows 7

Time Needed:
5 minutes

EFS is a Windows security feature that goes beyond simply restricting access to your files and folders. It encrypts your files and folders so that even if someone gains unauthorized access to your network, they can't just go waltzing through your most sensitive data or your most closely guarded secrets. After you've set up EFS, it operates seamlessly and automatically to encrypt your files when they're stored on your hard disk and decrypt them when you need access to them. Depending on how much data you're encrypting, it may take some time for Windows to initially encrypt your files. Relax. You can continue working while Windows does its own thing. When your files and folders are encrypted, they'll appear in Windows Explorer in a different color than your other files. Other than that, you won't notice any real difference! EFS uses your Windows login credentials to automatically decrypt your files for you when you open them. You can open, save, delete, print, and modify your files and folders just as you always have. Follow these steps to set up EFS on an individual file or folder.

1. Right-click the file or folder you want to encrypt and click Properties.

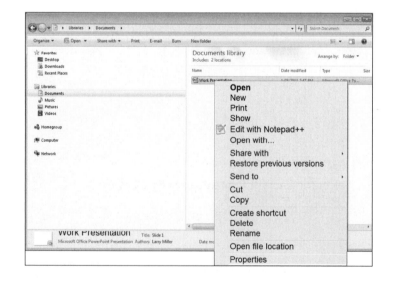

2. On the General tab, click the Advanced button.

3. Select the Encrypt Contents to Secure Data check box and click OK.

Creating and Backing up an EFS Certificate

Stuff You Need to Know

Toolbox:

✔ Computer running Windows 7

Time Needed:
20 minutes

Once you've set up EFS on your computer, you need to create a security certificate and key (password), and then associate it with your encrypted files. You will also need a way to recover encrypted data on your hard disk if your security certificate is deleted or corrupted. Otherwise, all is lost! To ensure you can always access your encrypted data, you should store a backup copy of your encryption certificate and key on a removable USB drive (along with your Windows Password Reset Disk; see Chapter 5). To create a security certificate, back it up, and associate it with your encrypted files, follow these steps:

1. From the Control Panel, click User Accounts and Family Safety.

2. Click User Accounts.

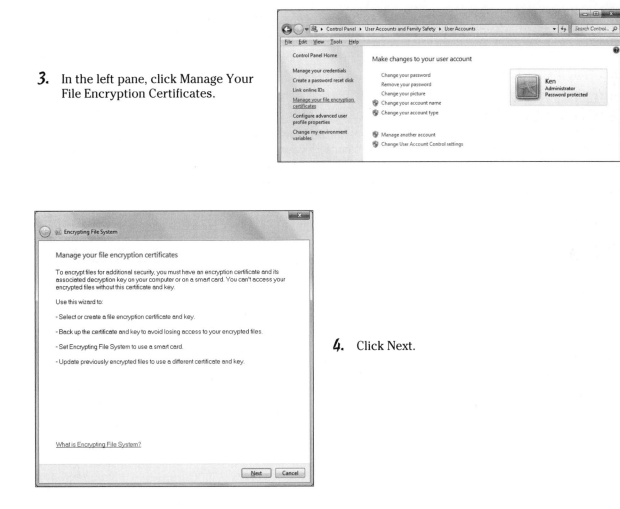

3. In the left pane, click Manage Your File Encryption Certificates.

4. Click Next.

5. Select Create a New Certificate and click Next.

6. Select A Self-Signed Certificate Stored on My Computer and click Next.

7. Windows creates a certificate for you. You can view the certificate by clicking View Certificate.

8. The certificate and its details are displayed on the various tabs. Click OK.

9. Select Back up the Certificate and Key Now and click the Browse button. Browse to the location you would like to store your certificate (preferably a removable USB drive). Give the certificate a name, create a password, and click Next.

10. Select the individual files and folders (or the entire drive) that you would like to associate with the newly created (and backed up) EFS certificate and key.

11. Windows updates your encrypted files and folders with the new certificate and key. This step will take some time depending on the amount of data that is encrypted.

Part V
The Part of Tens

The 5th Wave   By Rich Tennant

"Oh look! This must be one of those PCs that are assembled by prison inmates. It came bundled with a homemade shank in the mousepad."

In this part . . .

Ya know 'em; ya love 'em. These short chapters include helpful information to help you quickly find help, address issues joining a homegroup, and trouble-shoot problems when they arise.

Chapter 16

Ten Great Windows 7 Resources

Beyond networking, there are many exciting things to learn about Windows 7. In this chapter, I tell you about some great books and Web sites to help you in your quest for Windows 7 knowledge!

For Dummies Books

Okay, maybe there's a bit of shameless self-promotion here, but the For Dummies series really does provide some great resources to help you learn more about Windows 7 (and just about any other topic — technical or not — that you can imagine).

A few specific titles I recommend include

✔ Andy Rathbone's *Windows 7 For Dummies* (with DVD) and *Upgrading & Fixing Computers Do-It-Yourself For Dummies*

✔ Woody Leonhard's *Windows 7 All-in-One For Dummies*

✔ Nancy Muir's *Windows 7 Just the Steps For Dummies*

✔ Greg Harvey's *Windows 7 For Dummies Quick Reference*

For a book that's tailored more to older readers who may be new to technology and the Internet, Mark Justice Hinton's *Windows 7 For Seniors For Dummies* is a great resource.

For Dummies Web Site

In addition to the great For Dummies titles mentioned in the previous section, don't forget to check out the Dummies Web site (`www.dummies.com`) for expert tips, advice, and useful information, including how-to videos, step-by-step photos, thousands of articles, and Cheat Sheets.

Windows: The Official Magazine

```
www.officialwindowsmagazine.com
```

The Official Windows Magazine is the only computer magazine approved by Microsoft. It brings you all the latest information about Windows, such as details about new software and Windows versions, insider tips and tricks, and feature sections including "Discover" (Windows tips and Internet guides), "Explore" (tutorials), "Support" (technical advice and support), and "Upgrade" (reviews and recommendations).

The magazine is published monthly and is available in bookstores or by subscription.

Microsoft Web Site

```
www.microsoft.com
```

The Microsoft Web site is full of helpful Windows 7 resources, including tips and downloads, how-to's, online support, and much more. Particularly helpful, the "Windows 7 Help & How-To" section includes online tutorials, troubleshooting articles, how-to videos, community forums, blog posts, and much more.

MSDN and TechNet Web Sites

```
msdn.microsoft.com
technet.microsoft.com
```

Both the Microsoft Developer Network and Microsoft TechNet contain lots of great training resources, software downloads, technical support articles, Wiki communities, and blogs and forums.

Windows 7 News & Tips

www.windows7news.com

Windows 7 News & Tips was created in 2007 and is maintained by two Windows 7 enthusiasts. The site includes FAQs, screenshots, themes, wallpapers, guides, and more. You can learn about the different versions of Windows 7, watch videos, download drivers, read online guides and tutorials, and find performance tweaks and tips.

Windows 7 Forums

http://windows7forums.com

Windows 7 Forums (an independent Web site that is not authorized, sponsored, or endorsed by Microsoft, but is nonetheless an excellent resource!) includes discussion groups, blogs, and tutorials. The discussion groups include guides and how-to's on tweaks, customizations, and optimizing the user experience, along with support for installing and upgrading to Windows 7, networking, using associated software, and dealing with graphics issues, the Blue Screen of Death error, and hardware issues related to using the operating system.

There are also forums on the Web site for other operating systems, general computing, security topics, and software updates.

YouTube

www.youtube.com

YouTube is a great Web site for posting and viewing how-to video clips, but use it with caution. Just about anyone can post a video on YouTube, so some of the advice you get may not be safe or accurate. Still, the vast majority of videos posted provide good information, and you can learn a great deal.

Facebook

www.facebook.com

Facebook is a great social media Web site for learning more about Windows 7. There are Facebook pages specifically dedicated to Windows 7, and it's a great place to find other people and local user groups that may be able to help you figure out how to do something specific or solve a technical issue. For example, you might join the Windows User Community on Facebook. Just do a search in Facebook for Windows 7 and see what turns up!

Twitter

`www.twitter.com`

Believe it or not, there's a lot more to Twitter than keeping up with your favorite celebs' random rants and musings! A couple of tweets to follow include @windows 7center (`http://windows7center.com`), @theoscentral (`http://theoscentral.net`), and @Windows (`www.microsoft.com`). All of these Web sites have helpful discussion forums, tips and tutorials, downloads, screenshots, and much more.

Chapter 17

Ten Reasons You Might Not Be Able to Join a HomeGroup

The homegroup is a great new feature in Windows 7, making it extremely easy to share files, music, pictures, videos, and printers with just about anyone else on your home network. But occasionally, joining a homegroup can be a challenge. Here are a few possible reasons why you can't join a homegroup.

Verify a HomeGroup Exists on the Network

What do you do if a homegroup doesn't exist on your network? Okay, this may seem like the obvious "Is the power on?" question, but you should always start with the basics! See Chapter 6 to find out how to create a homegroup.

To create a homegroup, you must be running Windows 7 Home Premium, Ultimate, or Professional edition. Windows 7 Starter and Home Basic editions can only join an existing homegroup.

Ensure You Have a Network Connection

One reason you might not be able to join a homegroup is because you're not connected to the network. For help connecting to a wired network, see Chapter 3. To connect to a wireless network, see Chapter 4. See Chapter 18 for help troubleshooting your network connection. After you've connected to your network, you can join a homegroup.

Confirm You're Running Windows 7

You will be unable to join a homegroup if your computer isn't running Windows 7. Only Windows 7 computers can join a homegroup. Unfortunately, a computer running Windows XP, Vista, Mac OS, Linux, or any other operating system can't join a homegroup.

Make Sure the Network Location Isn't Set to Home

Another reason you may not be able to join a homegroup is because your network location isn't set to Home. A homegroup works only on a home network. To verify or change your network location, follow these steps:

1. **From the Control Panel, click Network and Internet.**

2. **Click Network and Sharing Center.**

3. **Under View Your Active Networks, verify the network that you are connected to is a Home Network as shown in Figure 17-1; if it isn't, click the network type that appears (either Public Network or Work Network).**

   If it is set to Home Network, keep troubleshooting.

Make sure the network is set to Home

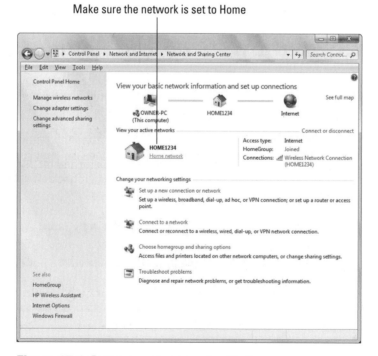

Figure 17-1: Ensure your network type is set to Home.

4. **In the Set Network Location dialog box that appears, click Home Network.**

5. **Your network location is changed to Home. Click Close.**

Check to See If the Computer Already Belongs to a HomeGroup

If your computer already belongs to a homegroup, it will not be able to join another homegroup. You can belong to only one homegroup at a time. If you find that you already belong to a homegroup but prefer to join a different homegroup, see Chapter 6 to learn how to leave a homegroup, then join a (different) homegroup.

Confirm That Someone Is Logged On to the Computer

You might not be able to join a homegroup if the computer on which the homegroup was created has been restarted, and no one has logged into it. Someone must log on in order for some required services for the homegroup to start.

Verify That HomeGroups Aren't Disabled

If you are using a computer that is part of a domain, your system administrator may have disabled homegroups. You will not be able to join the computer to a homegroup if this is the case.

Ensure Network Discovery Is Turned On

You will not be able to join a homegroup if network discovery is turned off. By default, network discovery is on. To verify that it is on, or to turn it back on, follow these steps (you can also see Chapter 7):

1. **From the Control Panel, click Network and Internet.**

2. **Click Network and Sharing Center.**

3. **In the left pane, click Change Advanced Sharing Settings.**

4. **Under Home or Work (Current Profile), click Turn On Network Discovery. Click Save Changes.**

If no options appear below Home or Work (Current Profile), click the down arrow to the right to expand the window and view the available options.

Confirm Peer Networking Grouping Service Is Running

If the Peer Networking Grouping service isn't running then you will not be able to join a homegroup. This service is required for a homegroup to function properly. To verify that this service is running, or to restart this service, follow these steps:

1. **From the Control Panel, click System and Security.**

2. **Click Administrative Tools.**

3. **Double-click Services.**

4. **Scroll down to Peer Networking Grouping and verify that its status is Started.**

5. **If it is not started (the status is blank), right-click Peer Networking Grouping and click Start from the drop-down menu as shown in Figure 17-2. You can also open the service properties for Peer Networking Grouping, change the startup type to Automatic, and then start the service to ensure it starts every time you turn your computer on.**

   Windows starts the service.

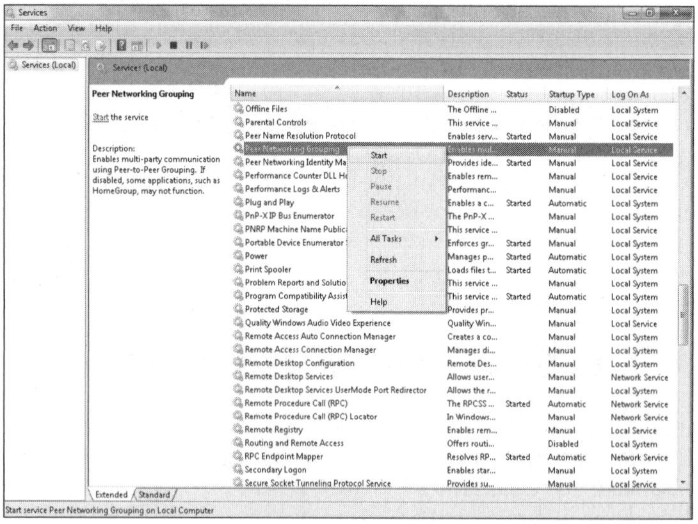

Figure 17-2: Start the Peer Networking Grouping service.

Make Sure the HomeGroup Provider Service Is Running

Another reason you may not be able to join a homegroup is because the HomeGroup Provider service may not be running. This service is required for a homegroup to function properly. To verify that this service is running, or to restart this service, follow these steps:

1. **From the Control Panel, click System and Security.**

2. **Click Administrative Tools.**

3. **Double-click Services.**

4. **Scroll down to HomeGroup Provider and verify that its status is Started.**

5. **If it is not started (the status is blank), right-click Peer Networking Grouping and click Start from the drop-down menu as shown in Figure 17-3. You can also open the service properties for Peer Networking Grouping, change the startup type to Automatic, and then start the service to ensure it starts every time you turn your computer on.**

   Windows starts the service.

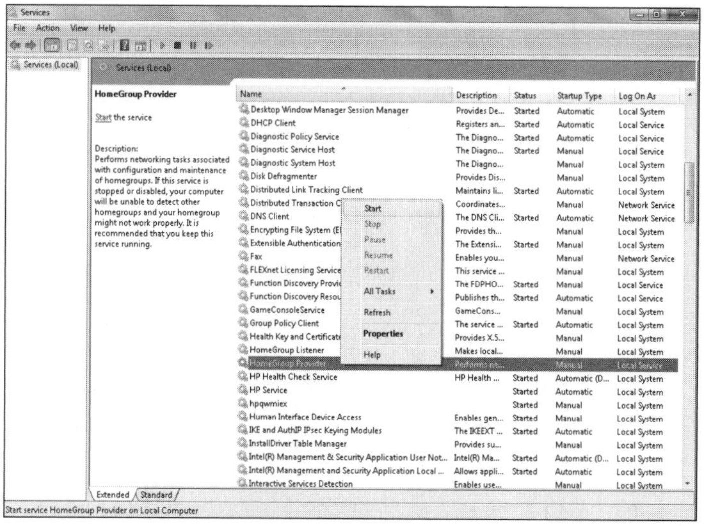

Figure 17-3: Start the HomeGroup Provider service.

Chapter 18

Ten Network Troubleshooting Tools

I f you're an experienced Windows user, trouble may seem like your middle name (well, at least your computer's). Fortunately, there are many tools to help you figure it all out! Here are ten great ones to get you started.

Running Windows Troubleshooters

Windows 7 includes several troubleshooting wizards (called *troubleshooters*) in the Action Center to help you resolve many common issues. When you're experiencing a problem and don't know what to do, run a troubleshooter to see if Windows 7 can help you identify and fix the problem. In the steps that follow, I tell you how to find the troubleshooters and walk you through running the Network Adapter (see Chapter 3 to learn about network adapters) troubleshooter as an example. You run the other troubleshooters in a similar manner.

1. **From the Control Panel, click System and Security.**

2. **Under Action Center, click Troubleshoot Common Computer Problems.**

3. **On the Troubleshooting screen, you can choose from several categories of troubleshooters including Programs, Hardware and Sound, Network and Internet, Appearance and Personalization, and System and Security. For this example, click Network and Internet.**

Microsoft regularly updates the troubleshooters in Windows 7. At the bottom of the Troubleshooting screen, make sure that this option is selected: Get the Most Up-to-Date Troubleshooters from the Windows Online Troubleshooting Service.

4. **Under the Network and Internet category, several troubleshooters are available. (See Figure 18-1.) For this example, click Network Adapter.**

Figure 18-1: Select the Network Adapter troubleshooter.

5. **In the Network Adapter troubleshooter window, click Advanced near the lower-left corner to choose whether Windows will apply repairs automatically. (The default is On.) Click Next.**

6. **The troubleshooter scans your computer to detect any problems.**

7. **If any potential problems are detected, the troubleshooter provides instructions for fixing the issue. Follow the instructions, and then click Check to See If the Problem Is Fixed to rescan your computer.**

   If the instructions that are provided do not address the problem you are experiencing, click Skip This Step to continue scanning for other problems.

8. **The troubleshooter summarizes the problems found and the status as shown in Figure 18-2. Click Close.**

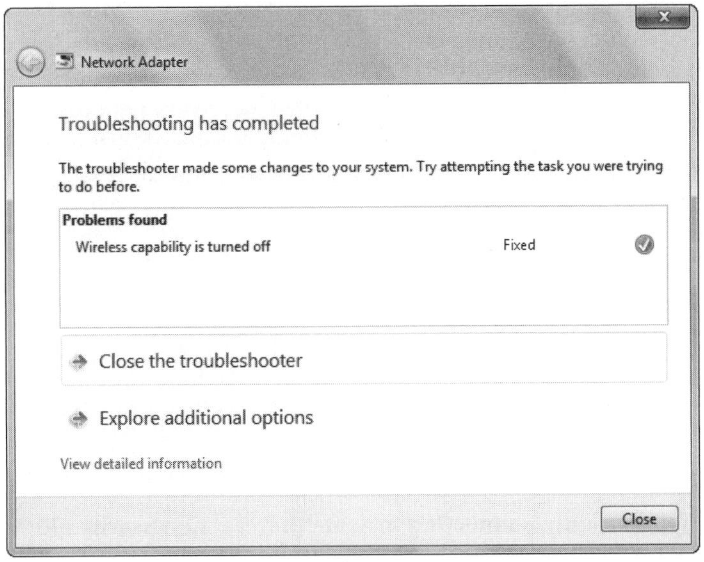

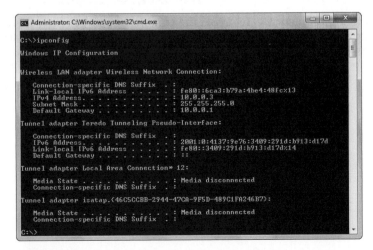

Figure 18-2: Review the troubleshooter's summary.

Troubleshooting with the ipconfig Command

The ipconfig command is a great networking troubleshooting tool that displays basic network information and allows you to reset or clear certain settings. To use ipconfig to reset your IP address or clear your DNS cache, follow these steps:

1. **Click the Start button, type** cmd **in the search window, and press Enter. This opens an MS-DOS command prompt window.**

2. **In the command prompt window, type** ipconfig **and press Enter. Depending on your computer networking hardware, you will see results for various adapters. (See Figure 18-3.)**

Figure 18-3: Review the results for the various adapters.

If you are connected to your network over a wired connection, look for configuration information under the network adapter you are using. If you are connected to a wireless network, check the settings under Wireless LAN Adapter Wireless Network Connection.

If the Media State is Media Disconnected, check your network cable (for wired networks), or verify that your wireless adapter and wireless access point are both turned on (for wireless networks). You should see some basic configuration information, including the IPv4 address, subnet mask, and default gateway.

See Chapter 2 to learn more about IP addresses, subnet masks, default gateways, and other networking basics. See Chapter 3 for more information on wired networks and Chapter 4 for more on wireless networks.

3. **If you do not see an IPv4 Address, Subnet Mask, or Default Gateway field, or if it appears incorrect, type** `ipconfig /release` **to clear your IP address configuration.**

4. **Next, type** `ipconfig /renew` **to reset your IP address information.**

5. **If you are having trouble connecting to some (but not necessarily all) Internet sites, try flushing the DNS cache by typing** `ipconfig /flushdns`.

DNS is the domain name system — the phonebook for the Internet. It translates easily remembered addresses like `www.microsoft.com` to cryptic IP addresses like `207.46.197.32` that computers and routers can recognize.

Ping!

One of the most basic yet useful network troubleshooting tools available to you is the ping command, which lets you test network connectivity. To use ping, follow these steps:

1. **Click the Start button and type** `cmd` **in the search window.**

    This opens an MS-DOS command prompt window.

2. **To verify that Windows 7 networking is actually working, type** `ping 127.0.0.1`.

    This is the loopback address (a virtual network adapter), and pinging it verifies that the IP stack (a set of communications protocols) in Windows 7 is functioning correctly. You should get four reply messages (think of it like a sonar ping) if everything is okay. (See Figure 18-4.) Otherwise, there is a problem with your Windows IP stack.

Figure 18-4: Verify that Windows 7 networking is working.

3. **To rebuild your IP stack, type** `netsh int ip reset c:\iprebuild.log`
   and restart your computer. You should also clear your DNS cache by typing
   the `ipconfig /flushdns` **command before restarting your computer. (See**
   the previous section.)

4. **Next, verify connectivity with your network adapter by pinging your com-**
   puter's IP address. (See the previous section for help determining your
   computer's IP address.)

   Type `ping` and the IP address of your computer — for example, `ping`
   `10.0.0.2`. You should get four reply messages if everything is okay.
   Otherwise, try disabling and re-enabling your network adapter, which I tell you
   how to do in the earlier "Running Windows Troubleshooters" section.

5. **Finally, verify connectivity with your default gateway by pinging its IP**
   address. (See the previous section for help determining your default gate-
   way address.)

   Type `ping` and the IP address of your default gateway — for example, `ping`
   `10.0.0.1`. You should get four reply messages if everything is okay. If you
   can't reach your default gateway, there could be a number of issues. Start by
   checking your router or wireless access point, and your computer's default
   gateway configuration.

Ping provides lots of other useful output beyond those described here. For example,
it can tell you the amount of time it takes for a *packet* (a block of data sent over an
IP-based network) to traverse your network (in milliseconds). If you get extremely
large or inconsistent results, there may be a latency issue on your network. Also,
look for dropped packets. (You don't get all four reply messages.) There are also
numerous variations of the ping command that are very helpful. Type **ping /?** to see
what other options are available.

Searching Google and Others

The Internet is chock-full of information to help you troubleshoot just about any computer or network problem you may be experiencing. But be forewarned; in addition to the multitude of well-meaning and knowledgeable resources available on the Internet, there are also plenty of well-meaning and not-so-knowledgeable, as well as not-so-well-meaning, sources of information on the Internet, and it can be difficult if not impossible to sort out the good, the bad, and the ugly.

To make the most of your Web searches, use a search engine such as Google, Yahoo!, or Bing and enter some specific information about the problem you are troubleshooting, not just *can't print*. For example, try *sharing printers in Windows 7* or enter a specific error message or code that your computer keeps displaying. Look for solutions and advice from Web sites that you are familiar with and trust, such as `ww.microsoft.com`. And always be sure you have a good backup of your computer and data before you attempt any troubleshooting in unfamiliar territory!

Viewing Problem Reports

Windows 7 keeps a detailed log of any problems your computer experiences (except EBKAC errors — error between keyboard and chair). To view the problem report, follow these steps:

1. **Click the Start button and type** `report` **in the search window. Click View All Problem Reports in the search results window.**

   This opens the Action Center and displays all sorts of problems you may not have even realized you had! You also get a summary of the problem and its status.

2. **Right-click any problem (on the screen) and click Check for a Solution (see Figure 18-5) to see if a solution is available, or View Technical Details for more information about the problem.**

Generating a System Health Report

The System Health Report provides a ton of details about your system, including warnings, basic system checks (which examine the operating system, disk, Action Center, system service, and hardware devices and drivers), performance, software and hardware configuration, and information about your CPU, network, interface, communications protocols (TCP, IP, UDP), disk, and memory.

TCP is the Transmission Control Protocol, IP is the Internet Protocol, and UDP is the User Datagram Protocol. All three are critical to network communications. See Chapter 2 to learn more.

To generate a System Health Report, follow these steps:

1. **From the Control Panel, click System and Security.**

2. **Click Action Center.**

3. **In the left pane, click View Performance Information. (See Figure 18-6.)**

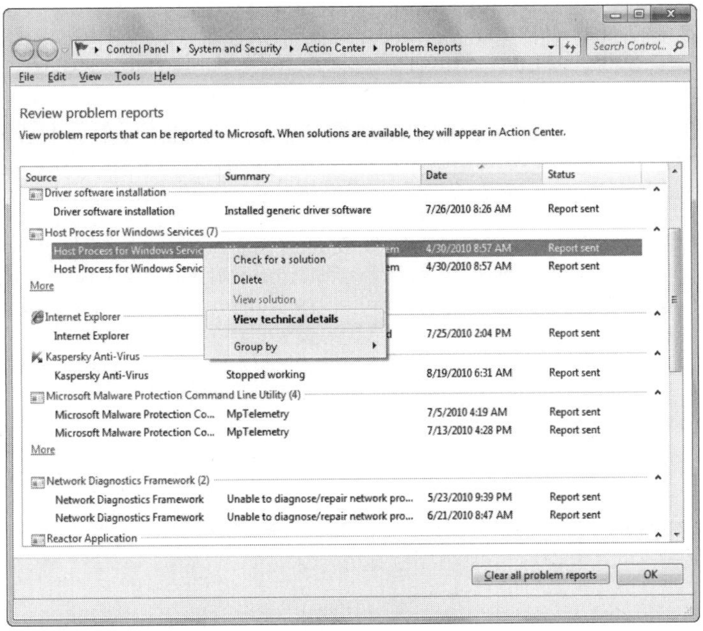

Figure 18-5: Check for solutions to a problem.

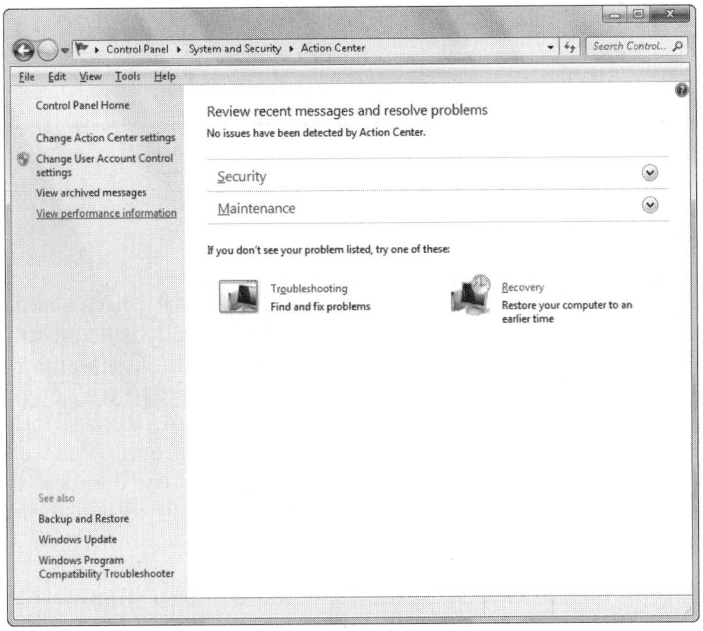

Figure 18-6: Using the Action Center to look at performance issues.

4. **In the left pane, click Advanced Tools.**

5. **Scroll to the bottom of the window and click Generate a System Health Report.**

6. **Windows scans your computer and collects data for approximately 60 seconds.**

7. **You can drill down into the various details of the resulting System Health Report for help in troubleshooting any number of problems you may be experiencing. (See Figure 18-7.)**

Figure 18-7: Review the results of the System Health Report.

Reliability Monitor

Windows 7 also includes a nice graphical utility that shows your system's stability over time, rated on a scale of 1 (bad) to 10 (good). There really is no specific threshold for when you need to take corrective measures, but the Reliability Monitor does show you the relative impact of a change you make to your computer, such as installing new hardware, upgrading software, or installing a new Windows security patch. If you notice your computer doesn't seem to be running as well as it used to, but aren't really sure when the problems started, take a look at the Reliability Monitor for some possible clues. To view the Reliability Monitor, do the following:

1. **Click the Start button and type** `reliability` **in the search window. Click View Reliability History in the search results window.**

   This opens the Action Center and displays the Reliability Monitor. (See Figure 18-8.)

2. **View the graph by Days or Weeks by clicking the appropriate link at the top-left corner of the graph, travel back and forth in time (at least to the present)**

by clicking the arrows on the left or right side of the graph, and most importantly, view detailed information about an event and check for possible solutions by clicking the corresponding day for that event.

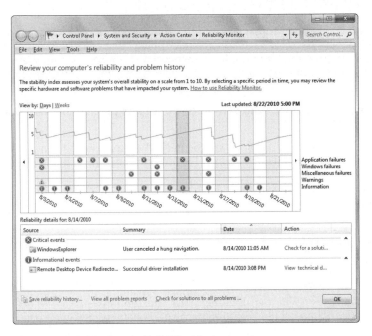

Figure 18-8: Viewing the Reliability Monitor results.

Creating a Play-by-Play with Problem Steps Recorder

The Problem Steps Recorder (PSR) is a great new troubleshooting tool in Windows 7 that lets you make a movie of your problem so that you can watch it over and over for hours of nonstop entertainment! Actually, the PSR makes it easy for you to send a play-by-play account of your problem to someone who can help you figure it out, using Internet Explorer to view the file. Here's how to use the PSR:

1. **First, you need to be able to re-create the steps that led to the problem you are experiencing. After you recall exactly how you did it (write it down, if necessary), click the Start button, type** psr **in the search window, and press Enter.**

2. **This opens the Problem Steps Recorder (see Figure 18-9); click Start Record. The PSR begins recording, and Recording Now flashes in the title bar.**

3. **You can pause the recording by clicking Pause Record.**

4. **You can also add a comment for the person who will view the recording, by clicking Add Comment. This pauses the recording, dims your screen, and opens a window for you to enter comments. Click OK to save the comment and resume recording.**

Figure 18-9: The Problem Steps Recorder.

5. **When you're done recording, click Stop Record. The Save As dialog box appears. Name the file and click Save. By default, Windows saves the recording to your Desktop as a compressed, .zip, file.**

6. **Send the file to the person who will help you (or copy it to a disc and take it to your favorite geek).**

When your helper unzips the file, it will be in MHT format, which is a proprietary Microsoft Web archive file format. The file can be viewed using Internet Explorer.

Getting Help from a Friend with Remote Assistance

Remote Assistance is your Windows lifeline. It lets you "phone a friend" when you're stuck and need help. Of course, Remote Assistance assumes you have a friend who knows at least a little more about your networking and computer troubles than you! If you don't have any friends of that ilk, you may need to pay someone to help you out.

Remote Assistance lets your friend (or helper) see your screen and even take control of your computer (if you allow it) so that she can help you quickly fix your problem. To use Remote Assistance, follow these steps:

1. **Click the Start button and type** remote **in the search window. Click Windows Remote Assistance.**

2. **Click Invite Someone You Trust to Help You. (See Figure 18-10.)**

If you get an error message stating that the computer isn't set up to send invitations, click Repair. This usually resolves the issue and allows you to use Remote Assistance.

3. **If you and your friend/helper are both using Windows 7, click Use Easy Connect. Otherwise, you need to choose either Save This Invitation as a File and give it to her on a disk or send it to her using a Web-based e-mail account (such as Hotmail or Yahoo!) or Use E-mail to Send an Invitation using an e-mail program such as Microsoft Outlook.**

For this example, click Save This Invitation as a File.

4. **Give the file a name and click Save. Windows saves the invitation as an RA Invitations (.msrcIncident) file.**

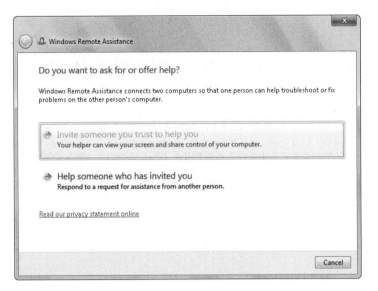

Figure 18-10: Inviting someone to help troubleshoot or fix a problem.

5. **Windows displays a password and waits for the incoming connection. You need to let your friend/helper know the password, preferably over the phone.**

Unless you have absolutely no other alternative, don't send the password via e-mail and *definitely* not in the same e-mail that contains the invitation. If the e-mail is intercepted, someone can pretend to be your friend/helper, connect to your computer, steal all of your personal information (and pictures), and do lots of damage to your computer (and finances, and reputation, and on and on)!

6. **When your friend/helper opens the invitation, she is prompted to enter the password and connect to your computer. (If you clicked Use Easy Connect in Step 3, your friend/helper doesn't need the invitation file; she can just start Remote Assistance on her computer and enter the password you provided.) You will then be asked if you would like to allow the connection. Click Yes.**

7. **Your screen will momentarily go black, and then reappear with a Windows Remote Assistance window letting you know your helper can see your desktop.**

8. **If your friend/helper needs to take control of your computer, she will click Take Control on her computer. You will be asked if you would like to share control of your desktop. Click Yes.**

You will be able to watch everything your friend/helper is doing while she has control of your computer. Your keyboard and mouse will still be active, so you can interrupt at any time, or just sit back and enjoy the show!

9. **When your friend has fixed your problem (or given up), you can stop Remote Assistance by clicking Stop Sharing. Close Remote Assistance by clicking the red X in the upper-right corner.**

Until you actually close Remote Assistance by clicking the red X, your friend/helper will be able to see a frozen image of your screen as it appeared when you clicked Stop Sharing.

TIP

Your invitation is valid for only 6 hours, after which it automatically expires.

Consulting Windows Help and Support

And last but not least — well, perhaps least; I'll let you decide — there's Windows Help and Support. To access it, click the Start button and click Help and Support, conveniently located just above Shut Down in case you're about to give up or already know that bit of sage wisdom for seemingly 99 percent of all Windows problems — reboot!

Index

Business/Accounting & Bookkeeping

Bookkeeping For Dummies
978-0-7645-9848-7

eBay Business
All-in-One For Dummies,
2nd Edition
978-0-470-38536-4

Job Interviews
For Dummies,
3rd Edition
978-0-470-17748-8

Resumes For Dummies,
5th Edition
978-0-470-08037-5

Stock Investing
For Dummies,
3rd Edition
978-0-470-40114-9

Successful Time
Management
For Dummies
978-0-470-29034-7

Computer Hardware

BlackBerry For Dummies,
3rd Edition
978-0-470-45762-7

Computers For Seniors
For Dummies
978-0-470-24055-7

iPhone For Dummies,
2nd Edition
978-0-470-42342-4

Laptops For Dummies,
3rd Edition
978-0-470-27759-1

Macs For Dummies,
10th Edition
978-0-470-27817-8

Cooking & Entertaining

Cooking Basics
For Dummies,
3rd Edition
978-0-7645-7206-7

Wine For Dummies,
4th Edition
978-0-470-04579-4

Diet & Nutrition

Dieting For Dummies,
2nd Edition
978-0-7645-4149-0

Nutrition For Dummies,
4th Edition
978-0-471-79868-2

Weight Training
For Dummies,
3rd Edition
978-0-471-76845-6

Digital Photography

Digital Photography
For Dummies,
6th Edition
978-0-470-25074-7

Photoshop Elements 7
For Dummies
978-0-470-39700-8

Gardening

Gardening Basics
For Dummies
978-0-470-03749-2

Organic Gardening
For Dummies,
2nd Edition
978-0-470-43067-5

Green/Sustainable

Green Building
& Remodeling
For Dummies
978-0-470-17559-0

Green Cleaning
For Dummies
978-0-470-39106-8

Green IT For Dummies
978-0-470-38688-0

Health

Diabetes For Dummies,
3rd Edition
978-0-470-27086-8

Food Allergies
For Dummies
978-0-470-09584-3

Living Gluten-Free
For Dummies
978-0-471-77383-2

Hobbies/General

Chess For Dummies,
2nd Edition
978-0-7645-8404-6

Drawing For Dummies
978-0-7645-5476-6

Knitting For Dummies,
2nd Edition
978-0-470-28747-7

Organizing For Dummies
978-0-7645-5300-4

SuDoku For Dummies
978-0-470-01892-7

Home Improvement

Energy Efficient Homes
For Dummies
978-0-470-37602-7

Home Theater
For Dummies,
3rd Edition
978-0-470-41189-6

Living the Country Lifestyle
All-in-One For Dummies
978-0-470-43061-3

Solar Power Your Home
For Dummies
978-0-470-17569-9

Internet

Blogging For Dummies,
2nd Edition
978-0-470-23017-6

eBay For Dummies,
6th Edition
978-0-470-49741-8

Facebook For Dummies
978-0-470-26273-3

Google Blogger
For Dummies
978-0-470-40742-4

Web Marketing
For Dummies,
2nd Edition
978-0-470-37181-7

WordPress For Dummies,
2nd Edition
978-0-470-40296-2

Language & Foreign Language

French For Dummies
978-0-7645-5193-2

Italian Phrases
For Dummies
978-0-7645-7203-6

Spanish For Dummies
978-0-7645-5194-9

Spanish For Dummies,
Audio Set
978-0-470-09585-0

Macintosh

Mac OS X Snow Leopard
For Dummies
978-0-470-43543-4

Math & Science

Algebra I For Dummies
978-0-7645-5325-7

Biology For Dummies
978-0-7645-5326-4

Calculus For Dummies
978-0-7645-2498-1

Chemistry For Dummies
978-0-7645-5430-8

Microsoft Office

Excel 2007 For Dummies
978-0-470-03737-9

Office 2007 All-in-One
Desk Reference
For Dummies
978-0-471-78279-7

Music

Guitar For Dummies,
2nd Edition
978-0-7645-9904-0

iPod & iTunes
For Dummies,
6th Edition
978-0-470-39062-7

Piano Exercises
For Dummies
978-0-470-38765-8

Parenting & Education

Parenting For Dummies,
2nd Edition
978-0-7645-5418-6

Type 1 Diabetes
For Dummies
978-0-470-17811-9

Pets

Cats For Dummies,
2nd Edition
978-0-7645-5275-5

Dog Training For Dummies,
2nd Edition
978-0-7645-8418-3

Puppies For Dummies,
2nd Edition
978-0-470-03717-1

Religion & Inspiration

The Bible For Dummies
978-0-7645-5296-0

Catholicism For Dummies
978-0-7645-5391-2

Women in the Bible
For Dummies
978-0-7645-8475-6

Self-Help & Relationship

Anger Management
For Dummies
978-0-470-03715-7

Overcoming Anxiety
For Dummies
978-0-7645-5447-6

Sports

Baseball For Dummies,
3rd Edition
978-0-7645-7537-2

Basketball For Dummies,
2nd Edition
978-0-7645-5248-9

Golf For Dummies,
3rd Edition
978-0-471-76871-5

Web Development

Web Design All-in-One
For Dummies
978-0-470-41796-6

Windows Vista

Windows Vista
For Dummies
978-0-471-75421-3

Available wherever books are sold. For more information or to order direct: U.S. customers visit www.dummies.com or call 1-877-762-2974.
U.K. customers visit www.wileyeurope.com or call (0) 1243 843291. Canadian customers visit www.wiley.ca or call 1-800-567-4797.